# Introduct

**T**he historic Roman city of Chester, ly is one of the most stunning cities in Bri the river's strategic importance and buil the wide estuary. For many centuries the estua route with Chester as it's main port and trading centre. By the 15thC silting made it difficult for ships to reach the city. This led to a succession of new ports developing in turn along the Wirral coast. In 1737 a new channel over 7 miles long, known as the New Cut, was opened. Its purpose was to revive Chester's fortunes as a port but it started a new chapter in the estuary's history. The canalisation of the river diverted its course to the Welsh side of the estuary, leading to the eventual demise of the principal Wirral port of Parkgate, whilst bringing trade and prosperity to Flintshire. Connah's Quay later became the major port, shipbuilding flourished and many industries developed alongside the river.

The Dee estuary serves as a natural boundary between England and Wales. It is an internationally renowned and protected Nature Reserve, with its mudflats and saltmarshes providing feeding and roosting for thousands of wading birds and wildfowl.

Over the centuries the estuary has witnessed Roman soldiers passing by on their way to Deva, troops embarking on campaigns by English kings against the Welsh and Irish, magnificent sailing boats plying their trade between Chester and Europe, passenger ferry services across the Dee, and in the early 20thC, coastal sailing ships, tugs, barges, and steamers built locally.

The 26 walks in this book explore Chester and both sides of the Dee estuary, including its fascinating maritime and industrial past. There are walks along ancient city walls, on canal towpaths, by the river, through woodland, dunes, on clifftops and beach, with stunning estuary views. They visit ancient castles, old ports, attractive villages, maritime relics, Heritage Parks and nature reserves.

The routes follow public rights of way or permissive paths and include sections of the new Wales Coast Path, and popular recreational routes such as the Wirral Way, Chester's Riverside Promenade and the Connah's Quay – Chester Railway Path. Many individual routes contain shorter walk options and can easily be linked with others to provide longer day walks, if required. Walking boots are recommended, along with appropriate clothing to protect against the elements.

Each walk has a detailed map and description which enables the route to be followed without difficulty. Bear in mind though that changes in detail can occur at any time. The location of each walk and a summary of their key features is provided. This includes an estimated walking time, but allow more time to enjoy the scenery.

Please observe The Country Code. *Enjoy your walking!*

# CHESTER CITY WALLS

**DESCRIPTION** A delightful and informative 2 mile walk following the ancient city walls anti-clockwise around the heart of this historic city passing many places of interest. Allow about 1½ hours.
**START** Chester Visitor Information Centre/ Town Hall [SJ 405664].

*T*he sandstone city walls, a Scheduled Ancient Monument, are the most complete circuit of Roman and medieval defensive town walls in Britain, and regular information boards trace their history. Built by the Romans to replace the original wooden defences of the Deva fortress, they continued to play a key role in subsequent periods of Chester's history, before becoming a fashionable promenade in the 18thC.

**I** Go past the imposing Victorian town hall then at the first road turn RIGHT past a booth and through Abbey Gateway opposite – *a vaulted mid 14thC sandstone archway, once the main entrance to St Werburgh's Abbey* – into Abbey Square, fronted by fine mid-18thC Georgian terraced houses. At the opposite side go along Abbey Street. At its end go up steps onto the city walls. Turn LEFT, soon passing King Charles Tower (**A**) then bending west above the canal – *built from Chester to Nantwich in the 1770s*. After crossing Northgate (**B**) continue along the walls past Morgan's Mount (**C**) to Bonewaldesthorne's tower (**D**) at the north western corner of the walls. *This tower protected the port, when the river Dee flowed near the western walls. However the river steadily receded, and the nearby Water Tower, when it was built in 1322 connected to the city walls by a spur wall, then marked the river's edge, but now stands some distance from it.* Continue south along the walls, over the railway, then descend to continue on the pavement alongside the walls overlooking Water Tower Gardens. Shortly, go up across Watergate (**E**) and continue beside the city walls, on the original river cliff, overlooking the racecourse, shortly passing the remains of the original Roman harbour wall (**F**). *In Roman times this area was a tidal pool and was later named after a small medieval stone cross (Rood), whose base is clearly visible. The racecourse, dating from the 16thC, is the oldest in the country.*

**2** Cross the main road at the Pelican crossing and continue along the city walls signposted to Bridgegate, adjoining Castle Drive. *Nearby is Chester Castle, built between 1788–1822 on the site of the original Norman motte and bailey castle of 1070 which protected the bridge over the Dee and the port.* Soon you bend left and descend to Castle Drive. Cross the road and follow the pathway above the river towards the 14thC Old Dee Bridge (see Walk 5 for information on the bridge). Recross Castle Drive to an information board on Shipgate (**G**), then go up steps on to the walls signposted to Eastgate, soon passing above The Groves – *Chester's popular riverside walkway – offering a good view of the river and its 11thC weir. Across the river, Handbridge was known as 'Treoeth' or burnt town, because it was so often set on fire by the Welsh during frequent clashes with the English.*

**3** The walls then bend away from the river to pass above Roman Gardens (**H**) – *the site of a clay tobacco pipe factory (1781–1917), making Chester centre of a flourishing industry, exporting great quantities. nearby Park Street are six timber and sandstone cottages (**I**), built as almshouses in the mid 17thC. (Just before Newgate you can descend steps to road level to visit both the Gardens and the nearby Roman amphitheatre, the largest ever found in Britain).* Continue with the walls across Newgate (**J**) then Eastgate (**K**) with its ornate clock *– designed to commemorate Queen Victoria's Diamond Jubilee and probably Chester's best known and photographed landmark. Here you can enjoy a good view along Chester's main shopping street.* Soon afterwards leave the walls and go down steps on the left past the Bell Tower – *built in 1975 to house the Cathedral's 13 bells* – and continue to the

0 _____ ¼
mile

N

Water Tower

canal

C B A

Bus Station

Cathedral

Bell Tower

Town Hall

i

①

K

J

Roman Amphitheatre

I H

③

E

CHESTER

Racecourse

Roodee

F

②

A483

Castle

P

G

Old Dee Bridge

River Dee

Handbridge

nearby road and past the impressive Cathedral – *originally founded in 1092 as a Benedictine abbey dedicated to St Werburgh and becoming a cathedral in 1541* – back to the start.

Old Dee Bridge

## WALK 2

# CHESTER WATERWAYS

**DESCRIPTION** A fascinating 3½ mile walk around the centre of Chester, featuring its two main waterways, the canal and the river Dee, which played key roles in the city's commercial and trading importance. After a short section of the canal the route heads via Grosvenor park to join the popular Riverside Promenade, which it follows past historical bridges and the Roodee, famous for its racecourse, to the Old Port of Chester, where it rejoins the canal. Note that the Roodee section of the Promenade will be closed during race days, but an alternative route is shown.

**START** Chester Visitor Information Centre/ Town Hall [SJ 405664].

*B**y the Middle Ages** Chester had become a thriving sea port, maritime centre and strategic gateway for government and trading links with Ireland, and had an important wine trade with France and Spain. Exports included leather goods, Cheshire salt, Welsh cattle and sheep, and even slaves! Local coastal trade was important, especially for supplying the North Wales castles. From the 15thC silting became an increasing problem, which prevented larger boats reaching Chester. In 1737, the New Cut was opened. The ambitious diversion of the course of the Dee to the Welsh side of the estuary was aimed to revive Chester's fortunes as a port. Unfortunately its benefits were short-lived, and the arrival of the canal connecting the Dee at Chester with Nantwich in 1779 failed to stop its decline as a port, with trade going to the emerging Liverpool. However, Chester's fortunes revived after the canal was extended to Ellesmere Port in 1795, providing a thriving trading link with the Mersey. By 1920 Chester had ceased to be an active port.*

**I** Go past the town hall and along Northgate Street. Just before Northgate turn LEFT along Water Tower Street, then go through an archway in the city walls opposite Canning Street and follow a path down to the canal towpath. Turn RIGHT along the canal through an impressive sandstone cutting crossed by two bridges. *The narrow 'Bridge of Sighs' was built in 1793 to enable prisoners from the gaol to visit a chapel on the opposite side for prayers before being hanged.* Continue along the canal, shortly passing under bridge 123E near the Lock Keeper pub – *previously the site of a timber yard. The next section of the canal was, during the 19th and early 20thC, a busy industrialised area, lined with warehouses and mills serviced by many narrow boats. It is now a fashionable part of the city following the conversion of old buildings for commercial and accommodation use.* Pass under a modern road bridge and enclosed footbridge by the Mill Tower Spa. After passing under bridge 123C ahead can be seen the Steam Mill – *a former flour mill and seed warehouse. On the opposite side of the canal stands Britain's only remaining Lead Shot Tower, which produced shot for muskets during the Napoleonic Wars in the early 1800s.* Go past under bridge 123B and past The Old Harkers Arms.

**2** Turn RIGHT along Steam Mill Street. At the main road turn RIGHT and cross the dual carriageway by the pelican crossing. Go down nearby Dee Lane, then enter the corner of Grosvenor Park. Go along the main pathway, then take the third pathway on the right to a statue of Richard, Second Marquis of Westminster – *the patron of this fine Victorian park which he created from fields in 1867.* Turn LEFT to a large viewing area overlooking the river, then descend steps on the right and follow the pathway along the edge of the park. Soon, turn LEFT down steps to a gate onto the bend of a road. Follow it down to the river then continue along The Groves – *a popular riverside promenade originally created in the early 18thC –* under the suspension bridge, past the bandstand and on to the end of the 14thC Old Dee Bridge. (See Walk 5 for more information.) Continue along Castle Drive opposite. *Alongside the bridge is the former hydro-electric power station, built in 1913 on the site of the Dee Mills, making Chester the first British city to generate hydro electricity. In 1951 it became a water pumping*

4

station. Follow the pathway above the river. *This section of riverbank once had a flourishing leather industry, which during the 17thC employed a fifth of the local population.*

**3** Continue along the edge of Little Roodee car park (café/toilets). Pass under the Grosvenor Bridge to enter the Roodee. *Opened in 1832, it was the largest of its type in the world with a single span of 200 feet that allowed masted ships to pass upriver.* Follow the riverside promenade past the racecourse. *In Roman times this area was a tidal pool and was later named after a small medieval stone cross (Rood), whose base still remains. The racecourse, dating from the 16thC, is the oldest in the country.* Pass under the railway bridge – *built in the 1840s* – and continue along the riverside promenade past apartments and New Crane Wharf, with its old warehouse, where the walkway is built directly above the former quay of the

Old Port. *Sea-going vessels up to 350 tons berthed here after the second half of the 18thC.* Go past the riverside frontage of modern apartments, then follow a pathway between them to the road. Turn LEFT to the nearby Dee Lock. *The river was originally connected to the canal at Tower Wharf through a large tidal basin. In 1801 this lock was built to enable boats in the basin to remain afloat at low tide.*

**4** Cross the road and go along the side of the modernised canal basin, past a liftbridge and round the side of canalside apartments to go up steps to a road. Turn RIGHT along the pavement opposite, then go through a kissing gate and down to the large canal basin of Tower Wharf. (See Walk 4 for information.) Turn sharp RIGHT and follow the towpath under the road and railway bridges, up past Northgate locks and under the modern road bridge to join your outward route. Take the stepped path angling RIGHT up to go through another archway in the walls. Go along Pemberton Road, then turn LEFT along King's Street to Northgate Street. Turn RIGHT back to the start.

# TOWER WHARF

**DESCRIPTION** A 5 mile walk exploring the northern part of Chester, featuring two interesting sections of the city's canal system and the large basin at its hub. Also a former railway line, now a designated recreational route, and Newton Hollows, a delightful ancient sunken green highway, once a Roman Road. Allow about 2½ hours.

**START** Chester Visitor Information Centre/Town Hall [SJ 405664].

*Tower Wharf stands at the junction of two canals. The Chester – Nantwich Canal, which opened in 1779, was initially a commercial failure, but its extension to Ellesmere Port during the 1790s turned Chester into a thriving trading and boat-building centre. From 1846 it was HQ of the Shropshire Union Railways and Canal Company , which owned over 400 narrow boats, flats and barges, most of which were built here. Between 1921-71 the boatyard was owned by the Taylor family and boat building and repair work continues to service today's recreational canal traffic.*

*Between 1795–1840, a popular horse-drawn passenger service operated daily between Tower Wharf and Ellesmere Port, from where passengers transferred to a Mersey packet which sailed to Liverpool. In 1801 about 15,000 people a year used this service.*

*Tower Wharf and the canal continue to be developed into a fashionable part of the city with attractive waterside businesses, bars, restaurants and apartments*

**I** Go past the town hall and along Northgate Street past the library. After the Pied Bull Hotel turn LEFT along King's Street, then RIGHT along Pemberton Road. Go through an archway in the city walls ahead and descend the stepped path to join the former Chester – Nantwich Canal. Turn LEFT along the towpath, under the road bridge and down alongside Northgate locks. *The staircase of three locks was changed from an original five locks in the 1790s.*

Continue under a railway and road bridge to reach Tower Wharf. *Opposite is Telford's Warehouse, built in the 1790s and now a popular music venue, bar and restaurant.* Follow the path alongside the large basin. *The lower basin (William's Moorings) was the short branch of the Ellesmere canal which connected via a tidal basin then lock, to the nearby River Dee.* Soon take its right fork past a covered dry dock, then cross the small 'roving bridge' over the canal – *designed to enable horses pulling boats to cross without needing to be unhitched.* After crossing a swing bridge by a small side basin go along the towpath past Taylor's repair yard opposite. Continue along the former Ellesmere canal, under two road bridges, past Chester University campus and over a road.

**2** At an old iron railway bridge turn RIGHT up to join the Chester to Connah's Quay railway path shared with National Cycle Route 5. *Opened in 1890, the former Mickle Trafford to Dee Marsh railway closed to passengers in 1969 and to freight in 1992. It served the former John Summers steel works at Shotton, and carried steel, coal, minerals, agricultural products. It is now a popular 'greenway'.* Follow it east, signposted to the city centre, over a road, then under two bridges. Continue along the tree-lined way, past the arched entrance to Northgate Ponds, over the railway line and a road. Pass under Newton Lane bridge, where there is a short cut option. Continue ahead signposted to Fairfield Road/Chester Zoo, soon passing along the edge of Lime Woods Fields recreational area.

**3** At a map/information board, ignore the continuing cycle/walkway to Mickle Trafford, but take the left fork towards Lime Field Park. At a crossroad of paths turn RIGHT signposted to Hoole Road. After crossing the nearby bridge turn RIGHT to follow a path down past an information board into Newton Hollows. Follow the tree-lined sunken way – *once a Roman Road from Deva to a manufacturing centre at Wilderspool (Warrington)* – to Elmwood Avenue to join Newton Lane. Follow it LEFT to Hoole Road then go along Hamilton Street opposite. At

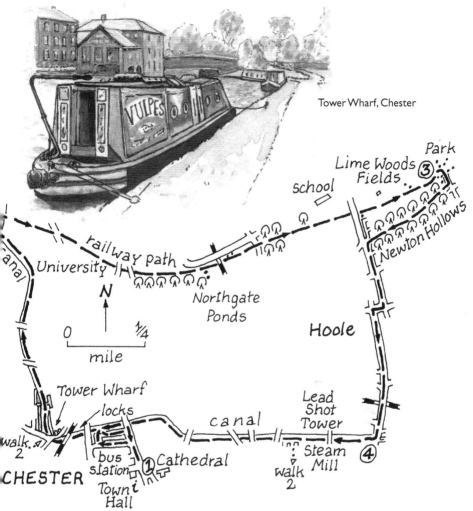

Tower Wharf, Chester

minor crossroads turn RIGHT along Panton Road, then LEFT along the right hand side of Westminster Road. At crossroads go up the road opposite to cross a footbridge adjoining the road bridge over the railway line. Continue along the pavement to cross over the canal.

**4** Descend to its towpath and follow the canal through what was once a busy industrialised area, lined with warehouses and mills, and now a fashionable commercial and accommodation area, with refreshment options. *On the opposite side of the canal stands Britain's only remaining Lead Shot Tower, which produced shot for muskets during the Napoleonic Wars in the early 1800s.* Follow the canal under several bridges, then through an impressive sandstone cutting featuring the narrow 'Bridge of Sighs' – *built in 1793 to enable prisoners from the gaol to visit a chapel on the opposite side for prayers before being hanged!* Soon afterwards you rejoin your outward route. Go up steps and take the path leading LEFT up to another archway in the city walls, then turn LEFT along Water Tower Street, then RIGHT along Northgate Street to the start.

# WAVERTON

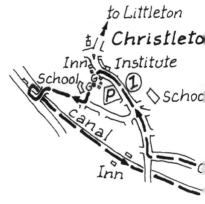

to Littleton

Christleto

Inn Institute

School

Schoo

Canal

Inn

**DESCRIPTION** A 6½ mile walk (**A**) through attractive countryside just east of Chester, featuring delightful canalside scenery. From Christleton the route follows the Shropshire Union Canal to Waverton and beyond. It then follows mainly field paths in a circuitous route back to Waverton, before a short section of canal on the return to Christleton. Allow about 3 hours. The route can easily be shortened to a 3½ mile walk (**B**) or undertaken as two separate circuits from Waverton.

**START** Christleton [SJ 443654] or Waverton [SJ 455642].

**DIRECTIONS** Approaching Christleton from the north via Littleton go through the village past the crossroads at St James Church, the Ring O' Bells, shops and Institute, to find a large parking area on the right. For the alternative start, turn off the A41 into Waverton to find a car park near the canal.

*The Chester – Nantwich Canal was built in the 1770s as a new transport solution to the gradual silting of the river Dee, which threatened Chester's importance as a trading and industrial centre. Initially it was a commercial failure, but fortunes improved with the canal's extension to Ellesmere Port in the 1790s and further works enabling links to the Midlands. This peaceful waterway is now part of the Shropshire Union canal.*

**1** Head north back through the village, then just past the Village Institute on the bend turn LEFT between Haulfryn and Styal cottage to a small waymarked gate. Follow the short enclosed path to another gate and round the perimeter of the primary school to a road. Follow it RIGHT. On the bend take a formal pathway to cross a nearby bridge over the canal onto the A41. Turn RIGHT to go through a gap at the end of buildings onto the canal towpath, which is shared with a cycle route. Follow the towpath back under the bridge and along the wide canal featuring canalside gardens, moored boats and overhanging weeping willow trees. Shortly you pass The Cheshire Cat, which

may entice you to stop, and a small boat repair yard. Go under bridge 120 and follow the canal through open country to pass under Egg bridge at Waverton. *Near the bridge was once a bustling commercial area hosting a rubber works, tile, cement and coal depots, as well as a flour mill, now residential apartments.* (For **Walk B** go through the adjoining car park and up onto the road, which you follow over the canal and through the village to point **3**.)

**2** Continue along the canal. The towpath is now narrower and no longer part of the cycle route. Pass under bridge 118 then bridge 117, known as Salmon's Bridge, where you leave the canal. Go up a path, across the bridge and along a tree-lined path. The path continues along the edge of two fields past a wood, then across three fields to a road. Follow it LEFT. At the junction turn RIGHT then take a signposted path on the left. Walk along the edge of a large field and across a footbridge over a stream Follow the path up the field to cross a small footbridge and stile. Go across the next field to a stile in the right hand corner. Follow the hedge on your right round to a stile/footbridge near the corner. Go along the edge of the next large field to a stile in the corner and footbridge beyond. Follow the next field edge to a stile onto a road. Follow it LEFT. At the junction keep ahead. After about 120 yards take a signposted path through a kissing gate on the left. Follow it across the field to go through a wide gap in the right hand corner and a gate beyond. Follow the kissing gated path across four fields, then an enclosed path to a nearby house and go along its tree-lined driveway to a road.

**3** Pass through a gap at the side of the gate opposite and continue to a kissing gate at a signposted path junction. Keep ahead and follow the path round the field edge, past a small pool and on to a gate. Continue along the field edge to a kissing gate in the corner to emerge from trees onto the canal. Follow the narrow path beside the canal and through a kissing gate. Shortly the path moves away from the canal to another kissing gate then crosses the next field to a further kissing gate. Go along the enclosed path, then a lane past houses to a road at the outskirts of Christleton. Follow it RIGHT past side roads and the entrance to Christleton High School to the start.

The canal near Christleton

## WALK 5

# ECCLESTON

**DESCRIPTION** A 6¼ mile (**A**) or 4½ mile (**B**) walk from Chester featuring one of the finest section of the River Dee, the attractive Eaton estate village of Eccleston, attractive woodland, and a Roman Shrine. Allow about 3½ hours. Starting from the car park at the site of the Eccleston ferry, which operated here from the mid-18thC until 1940, adds an extra ⅔ mile to the distance, and offers a shorter 2¾ mile walk (**C**).

**START** Old Dee Bridge, Chester [SJ 406658] or Eccleston riverside car park [SJ 415622].

*T*he *seven arched* stone Old Dee bridge was built in 1387, a successor to earlier wooden bridges that have stood here since the late 11thC, near the site of an earlier ford used by the Romans. The bridge was the only crossing over the river until the 19thC and important for trading and military purposes. Tolls regulated traffic across the bridge for centuries until they were abolished in 1885. The nearby 11thC weir provided water power for a corn-mill on the Chester side of the bridge, producing flour and oatmeal until the 19thC. Fulling mills for washing cloth were built on the south side of the weir. For centuries the weir was blamed for the silting of the river downstream, flooding and impeding salmon heading upstream to spawn, but survived all attempts at its removal. Steps now help migrating salmon to pass this barrier.

I At the southern side of the bridge turn LEFT down steps and go along the riverside path past a fish-pass and trapping house at the end of the weir – *used to tag and monitor the progress of salmon and sea trout to their spawning grounds above Llangollen. Salmon fishing is one of Chester's traditional industries. The river between the weir and the Dee bridge was known as 'King's Pool' – only the Abbott of Chester and his monks were allowed to fish in it. On the site of the nearby modern apartments used to be a tobacco and snuff factory built in the 1780s.* Continue under Queens Park suspension bridge – *built in 1923 to replace one from 1852 – and along the river to enter Earl's Eye Meadows – a popular open green space donated for recreational useage. Rowing on the river has been popular since the 18thC, with races between boatmen. Its later promotion as an athletic and innocent sporting pastime led to the establishment of Chester Victoria Rowing Club in 1838 – the oldest 'open' rowing club in Britain. In 1840 it was renamed the Royal Chester Rowing Club after receiving patronage from the Queen. Other local clubs followed, along with race prizes and betting, and amateur racing developed through the Chester Regatta which was held here.* Follow the riverside path along the edge of the Meadows, soon bending south past the ferry crossing point.

2 After leaving the Meadows the riverside path continues along the edge of a series of fields. Later the path passes a large pumping station then houses. *In Roman times there was a crossing here and a quay for discharging tiles and pottery from Holt, for transporting by cart to Deva to avoid the weir.* (For **Walk B** follow a waymarked path up the field edge to the road.) Continue on the riverside path to pass under the A55. *Eccleston, with its red sandstone church tower, is visible ahead. This section of the river was popular for boating trips in Edwardian times.*

3 After going through the first of two kissing gates, follow a path away from the river up to Eccleston. Go up the road. *A lane on your right leads to the churchyard, where members of the Grosvenor family – Duke and Duchesses of Westminster – are buried by the ruin of an earlier church.* Continue up the road past the entrance to St Mary's church, dating from 1899. *Note the early 18th wrought-iron gates made by the famous Davies brothers of Bersham.* At the road junction by a small 19thC stone shelter, keep ahead then turn RIGHT along Eaton Road, past the 19thC Primary School. Continue along the pavement out of Eccleston – *on the course of the Roman Road from Chester to Wroxeter* – soon passing over the busy A55. (Later, for **Walk C**, at the City of Chester sign go through a kissing gate and down the field

to join the riverside path.) Continue along the pavement to enter Handbridge district.

**4** About 50 yards after passing Green Bank road cross the road to go through a kissing gate at the end of the wood opposite. Follow the wide path back through the wood edge, shortly near the adjoining field, to join a wide formal path- way. *This is the Chester Approach, locally known as the Duke's Walk, the former carriage driveway which went from Chester to Eaton Hall, the home of the Grosvenor family, now broken by the A55.* Follow it RIGHT past then through, attractive mature woodland, past nearby Chester tennis club and a hospital, to reach the lodge by the large iron gated entrance. Here take a pathway on the left to nearby Wrexham Road. Turn RIGHT along the pavement by the extended roundabout, past traffic lights to cross Overleigh Road.

**5** Use the Pegasus crossing to cross both lanes of Grosvenor Road to a signposted path opposite. Go down the stepped path into the wood. Soon, at a crossroad of paths, turn RIGHT and follow the main path through the attractive woodland, shortly passing under a high iron footbridge. At the river turn RIGHT along a wide stony path under the nearby Grosvenor Bridge. *Opened in 1832, it was the largest of its type in the world with a single span of 200 feet that allowed masted ships to pass upriver.* Shortly, continue ahead along a rough lane then track to the bottom of two cobbled streets. Go through the ornate sandstone gateway into Edgar's Field Park *– reputed to be the site of King Edgar's 10thC Royal Palace.* Go up the right pathway, soon passing on your right the Shrine to the Roman Goddess Minerva. *It was carved into the face of the sandstone block by Roman soldiers who quarried sandstone outcrops here for building their fortress on the opposite side of the river.* Continue to the road by the 18thC Ship Inn at Handbridge near the Old Dee bridge.

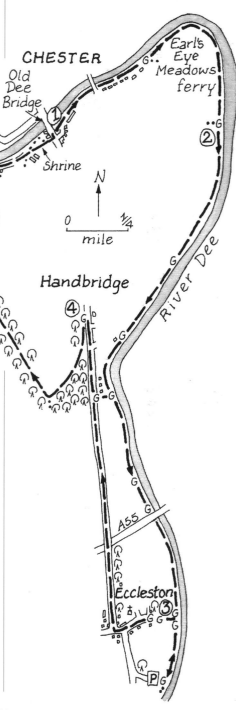

11

## WALK 6

# CHESTER OLD PORT

**DESCRIPTION** A 5 mile walk featuring both sides of the river Dee and the Old Port of Chester, which developed after the New Cut. The route follows the Dee Coastal Path then joins the Riverside Promenade at Chester Old Port. It crosses the river and passes through Curzon Park residential area to Saltney, before a final section of riverside walking. Allow about 2½ hours.

**START** Higher Ferry, Saltney Bridge [SJ 370659].

**DIRECTIONS** Leaving Chester on the A548 go past the Park & Ride, then turn left along Ferry Lane to the road end. Alternatively park on the southern side of the bridge by the B5129.

**1** Follow the embanked cycle/walkway alongside the river towards Chester, then go through the edge of Cop Park – *from where in the 18thC Cheshire cheese was exported to London* – and on to Sealand Road. Turn RIGHT to reach the Dee Lock – *built in 1801 to improve the link with the nearby canal basin.* Just beyond, go between apartment blocks and along their riverside frontage. Continue along the formal Riverside Promenade past New Crane Wharf, where the walkway is built directly above the former quay. *Sea-going vessels up to 350 tons berthed here after the mid 18thC. See Walk 2 for more information on Chester's maritime history.* Continue above the river to a gate (locked on race days – an alternative route shown). Pass under the railway bridge to reach the Roodee – *in Roman times*

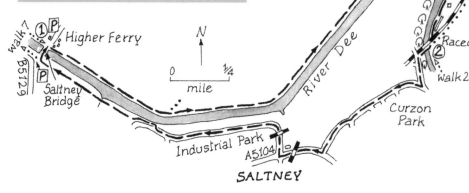

**S**ee *Walk 7 for information on the ferry. The arrival of the railway in 1846 saw extensive industrial development on the southern side of the river leading to the creation of Saltney as a thriving suburb of Chester. The Great Western Railway used tugs to tow up to 300 ton ships up river to its own wharf, where wheat and iron ore were offloaded and coal and flour exported. Between 1913–1935 there was a thriving shipbuilding yard at Saltney, which produced tugs, cargo ships, vehicular ferries, lightships, barges, hospital ships, and yachts.*

*a tidal pool. The racecourse, dating from the 16thC, is the oldest in the country.*

**2** Go up steps and follow the path by the railway bridge, then up steps onto a road. Follow it LEFT to a junction and turn RIGHT along Earlsway. After the road bends left, turn RIGHT along Mount Pleasant. At the main road in Saltney turn RIGHT, pass under the railway bridge, then turn RIGHT along River Lane. Follow the road through an industrial estate. Later join a wide cycle/walkway near the river to reach Saltney bridge.

The 1732 Act of Parliament that led to the canalisation of the Dee, known as the New Cut, also required the provision of two ferries linked to ancient trackways across the Dee marshes. Both had been established by 1740. Lower Ferry, at Queensferry, provided passage for passengers, animals, carts and carriage. Higher Ferry was for foot passengers only and operated until 1968 when the footbridge was built. In later years the ferry carried people from Blacon to work at the many Saltney-based industries, and children to school. In the 1950s an outboard motor replaced oar and muscle, and the boat was able to carry 15 people and push bikes. Bob Manifold was the last of several generations of the same family who worked the ferry.

The New Cut took four years to complete and involved digging a trench 80 feet wide and 8 feet deep by hand, with the help of horsepower – a major engineering feat of its day. About 1½ million tons of excavated spoil was used to form the north bank of the channel, which was pitched with stone. The New Cut was primarily aimed at improving Chester's sea-borne trade, but it also led to the reclamation of 2000 acres of desolate Saltney marshes, during the last quarter of the 18thC. The land was initially used for farming and later, industrial development on the southern side of the river.

**I** Cross the footbridge then head west along the flood embankment parallel with the river. Later you cross the Airbus' access road to the nearby quay. From here aeroplane wings are moved by barge along the river, then estuary to Mostyn Docks on their journey to Toulouse, France. Continue along the embankment to a stile in a large fence at an industrial estate. Follow the path away from the river, round a large building,

## WALK 7
# THE NEW CUT I

**DESCRIPTION** A 7½ mile walk along both sides of the river Dee, between two bridges on the site of ancient ferry crossing points. This straight, peaceful and little known canalised section of the river has a lot of history to tell. Allow about 3½ hours.
**START** Higher Ferry, Saltney Bridge [SJ 370659]. See Walk 6.

then between fences to a lane. Turn RIGHT along a wide stony track past industrial units, soon passing over a small inlet. The narrower rough track continues past chalets and beside the river to a house. Continue along the embankment. Later pass through girder posts by a gate and go along the tree-lined path ahead, then rough track past Riverside Joinery. At the bend of a road go past a barrier ahead to a small pumping station. Turn RIGHT and follow a narrow path beside the fence, under the 1960 road bridge above the river, and continue round the perimeter of Lindop Bros. Garage to the road at Queensferry.

**2** Turn RIGHT to cross the nearby Blue Bridge. (See Walk 20 for information on the bridge and Lower Ferry.) Now follow the wide surfaced Dee Coastal Path above the river back to Saltney BrIdge. By the mid-19th the waterfront opposite was a hive of activity, with warehouses, wharves and tramways linked to local collieries and the potteries at Buckley, enabling the export of coal, bricks, and tiles. Wharves also served a chemical works, wire works and an explosives factory. Shipbuilding flourished during the 19thC and a fishing fleet was based here. Early last century, the sea trade declined. During World War II wire hawsers were stretched across the river to prevent German aircraft landing on the Dee.

## WALK 8

# THE NEW CUT 2

**DESCRIPTION** A 3¾ mile walk along both sides of the river Dee between Connah's Quay and Queensferry, using cycle/walkways and paths. The route features the first section of the canalised Dee, known as the New Cut, and two historic crossing points of the river: Hawarden railway bridge that connected North Wales via the Wirral with Liverpool and the Blue Bridge at the site of an ancient ferry crossing. Allow about 2 hours. See *Walk 7 for more information on the New Cut.*

**START** Wepre Riverside car park, Dock Road, Connah's Quay [SJ 300698].

**DIRECTIONS** Head west through Connah's Quay and just as the road begins to rise you will find Dock Road on the right. Follow it through the industrial estate, soon alongside the river. Go under a barrier to the car park.

*A*fter the new channel *was opened in 1737 a stone pier and quay was built at the hamlet of Goftyn. By the early 19thC it had been developed by the Irish Coal Company into a thriving port, from where ships sailed regularly to Liverpool, London, Dublin and parts of North Wales. Shown as 'New Quay' on late 18thC maps, by 1839 it was renamed Connah's Quay, possibly after an Irish merchant or landlord at the Old Quay House.*

*Its later prosperity was then largely due to the export of tiles and bricks directly from Buckley by a single track railway which opened in 1862. It also became an important shipbuilding centre, with Ferguson, McCallum & Baird building steamers and three-masted sailing vessels between 1859-1917, and James Crichton's yard producing a diverse range of small boats. During the late 19thC a fleet of coastal sailing ships traded to other ports in Britain and Europe. It became the main Dee port and was so busy that ships often berthed alongside each other whilst waiting to load or unload. It was one of the last British ports to own sailing ships. By the 1930s the port had declined due to silting and competition from Liverpool, and about 1960 the docks were closed.*

Join the nearby surfaced cycle/walkway at an information board and follow it east, soon bending away from the river to reach the former Connah's Quay railway line. After passing over the long narrow inlet, go through a kissing gate on the left. Follow the signposted Riverside Walk along the embankment on the eastern side of the inlet, shortly bending right towards Hawarden Bridge. Continue with the waymarked path to rejoin the cycle/walkway. Follow it to Hawarden Railway bridge. *William Gladstone, four times Prime Minister from Hawarden Castle, laid the first cylinder of this swing railway bridge in 1887. Two years later his wife Catherine opened it, allowing a flotilla of vessels to pass through to the cheers of spectators lining the banks. The bridge consists of two fixed spans, with a central 285 feet span that could be swung open in 30 seconds by two huge hydraulic rams, originally worked by steam driven pumps, later electrically driven. It has remained fixed since the 1960s.* Go up steps to cross the adjoining bridge over the river for walkers and cyclists.

**2** At the other side descend steps on your right and continue along the northern bank of the river, passing the elegant former John Summers Steel HQ (1908). *Along the northern side of the river are the remains of several wooden wharves associated with the once extensive iron & steel works of John Summers & Sons, now Corus, first established in 1896. During the 20thC it operated a fleet of vessels, many built locally, for transporting steel. At its peak In the late 1960s the plant had a workforce of over 13,000 people. In 1980 open-hearth steel-making dramatically ended with the loss of over 6,000 jobs.* Continue along the embanked path to reach the road near the Blue Bridge connecting Queensferry and Garden City. Turn RIGHT across the bridge. *The 1732 Act of Parliament that led to the canalisation of the Dee required the provision of a ferry here across the new channel linked to existing ancient trackways, and by 1740 Lower Ferry for passengers, animals, carts and carriages had been established. In 1820 it was named King's Ferry in honour of George IV's accession, then Queensferry in 1837 upon*

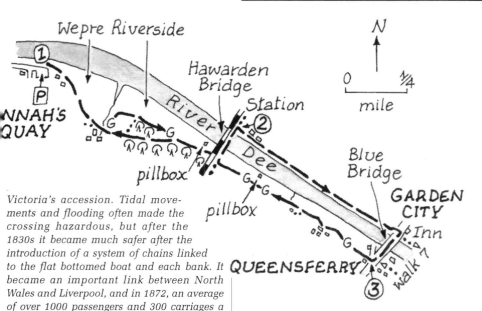

Wepre Riverside

Hawarden Bridge

Station

N

0 ────── ¼
mile

CONNAH'S QUAY

River Dee

pillbox

pillbox

Blue Bridge

GARDEN CITY

Inn

QUEENSFERRY

Victoria's accession. Tidal movements and flooding often made the crossing hazardous, but after the 1830s it became much safer after the introduction of a system of chains linked to the flat bottomed boat and each bank. It became an important link between North Wales and Liverpool, and in 1872, an average of over 1000 passengers and 300 carriages a week crossed here. The demise of the ferry came with the opening of the Jubilee Bridge in 1897. However, in 1926, due to increasing and heavier road traffic, it was replaced with the Blue Bridge, made of steel and with electric controlled mechanisms able to open or close it in 2½ minutes. The remains of the old bridge are still visible.

**3** Take a signposted path to Wepre Riverside along a rough stony track to a kissing gate/gate. Continue with the fading stony track along the field edge past a farm. When the track descends to a nearby utility building keep ahead along the grass embankment parallel with the river to a kissing gate. Continue to gates on the bend of a surfaced cycle/walkway. *Pillboxes are a feature of the river from Connah's Quay to Chester. They were sited at key locations in 1940 to provide defensive cover. They were made of reinforced concrete with 15 inch walls and 12 inch roof. Loophole openings provided 90 degree field of fire for each of five guns, and there was also an anti-aircraft gun mounting.* Keep ahead on the cycle/walkway towards Hawarden Bridge. At the signposted junction turn RIGHT to join your outward route by the bridge. Follow the cycle/walkway back to the start.

Blue Bridge, Queensferry

# EWLOE CASTLE & WEPRE PARK

**DESCRIPTION** A 3⅓ mile walk exploring the many delights of Wepre Park, featuring the remains of Ewloe Castle, and the adjoining countryside. Allow about 2 hours.

**START** Wepre Park car park [SJ 295684].

**DIRECTIONS** Wepre Park lies just off Wepre Drive and is signposted from the main road (B5129) in Connah's Quay and the B5126 from Northop.

*W*epre Park *is a beautiful historic wooded river valley – a hidden gem in the heart of Connah's Quay. Its 160 acres of ancient natural broadleaved woodland are all that remain of the once extensive Ewloe Forest. The Park, which provides an important habitat for a variety of wildlife, including the great crested newt, is part of Connah's Quay Ponds and Woodlands SSSI. For centuries Wepre was part of a large estate, boasting an ancient manor house, and a later Georgian Hall, where The Visitor Centre and café now stands. After a glorious, then chequered history, Wepre Hall was demolished in 1960 then developed into today's popular green space, now managed by Flintshire Countryside Service. A detailed leaflet on the Park and its history is available from the Visitor Centre.*

*The Park contains the remains of Ewloe Castle, said to have been built by the Welsh Prince Llewelyn ap Gruffudd in 1257 to protect the ownership of Ewloe Forest from English invaders. Its structure of two adjoining walled enclosures and towers, as well as its location, was inherently weak, indicating its function was more as a base for conducting border skirmishes. It was taken by English forces in 1877 as part of Edward I's protracted conquest of Wales and later abandoned.*

**I** From the large information board at the corner of the car park by the end of the skateboard park follow a narrow stony path past the perimeter of the children's play area down into the wooded valley to a crosspath near a footbridge over Wepre Brook. The route now turns sharp left along this path, but first stand on the bridge for a view of the nearby waterfall tumbling over a dam – *built to power a turbine for generating electricity in the Old Hall.* Now head northwards with the path near Wepre Brook to cross a large footbridge over it. Just beyond, take the wider right fork through the wood, past side paths and on above Wepre Brook at the edge of the wood. At a Wepre Park welcome board, turn RIGHT up a wide stony path between hedges. Just after it bends left, cross a stile on the right. Follow the path across the field to another stile, then angle LEFT across the next field past a waymarked telegraph pole to a stile by old gates.

**2** At a finger post just beyond, turn RIGHT up a wide hedge-lined farm track to a stile/gate. Continue up the hedge-lined green track, soon becoming a path and passing a stile on the left. Keep ahead with the enclosed path, soon becoming sunken in nature and continuing to gently rise. At a crosspath by a stile on the left, turn RIGHT past a waymarked post to a stile. Go along the left-hand field edge to an old kissing gate by a gateway in the corner. Follow the hedge on your right along the next large field then just beyond midway cross a stile in the hedge. Go across the field end to a kissing gate ahead onto an access lane. Go through a kissing gate opposite to re-enter Wepre Park. Now follow the wide path down through mature woodland. Shortly you pass a small reedy pond up on the right. *The spring feeding the pond was used by nearby Fox's brewery (1844 – 1950s).*

**3** Just beyond turn sharp LEFT down another path to a large footbridge over the stream and up through the trees. As it bends left descend a concrete stepped path on the right and continue with the path to the nearby ruins of Ewloe Castle. A flight of steps gives you access to the lower ward of the castle containing a well and West tower. Further steps allows you onto the upper ward. Follow the path bearing LEFT round the ruined Welsh tower to steps giving access to its top. Continue round the tower then descend the steps to rejoin the woodland path. Follow it beneath the castle wall to an information board near the ruined West Tower. Just beyond turn RIGHT to follow a part stepped path down through the wood to cross a large footbridge over Wepre Brook.

**4** Here take a footpath on the left (optional), signposted to Devil's Basin, which follows Wepre Brook past impressive crags opposite to a point overlooking a small waterfall above a pool, known as Devil's Basin. Retrace your steps to the Devil's Basin board, then go past the nearby stone bridge of Pont Aber – *built about 1800 on the site of an earlier bridge*

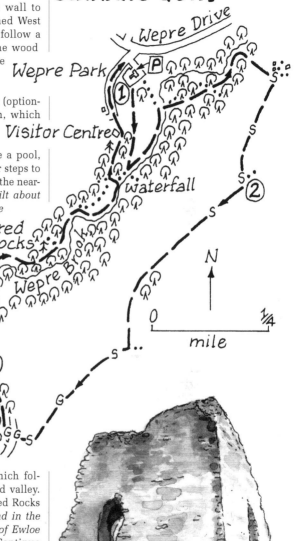

CONNAH'S QUAY

Wepre Drive

Wepre Park

Visitor Centre

waterfall

red rocks

Wepre Brook

N

0    ¼

mile

Devil's Basin Ewloe Castle

– and continue on a wide path which follows Wepre Brook down the wooded valley. Shortly you climb steps and pass Red Rocks – *an outcrop of red sandstone found in the Park and used in the construction of Ewloe Castle and other local buildings.* Continue with the wide path above the Brook, past picnic tables and a path rising left. Shortly, go down a stepped path on the right to follow a railed sleeper path beside the brook. Just before the dam turn LEFT up a stepped path to rejoin the wide main trail. Follow it RIGHT to the Visitor Centre and café, before returning past the large children's play area to the start.

Ewloe Castle

# SHOTWICK CASTLE

**DESCRIPTION** A 2¼ mile walk exploring part of historic Shotwick Park, featuring attractive woodland and the site of Shotwick Castle. Allow about 1½ hours.

**START** Church Way, Saughall [SJ 363704].

**DIRECTIONS** Church Way, where parking is available, lies just off the main road between All Saints Church, and the Junior School.

*Prior to the New Cut and the land reclamation schemes in the 18thC, Saughall stood at the edge of the former Dee coastline, and once had an anchorage for ships. This ancient settlement has long associations with the Earls of Chester and St Werburgh's Abbey. In 1327, Edward III, as Earl of Chester, created Shotwick Park as a Royal deer park, which was granted to a succession of royal favourites. In later centuries it fell under various ownerships, eventually becoming part of Cheshire County Farms estate, with access enjoyed by permissive paths. The Park was the royal manor of Shotwick Castle, which was built in the 11thC to defend the nearby major crossing point of the river Dee. The castle was used by English Kings during the 12th and 13thC as a base for campaigns in Wales and Ireland, after which it gradually fell into ruin.*

**I** Follow the road south westwards through the village to the distinctive clock tower on the library/institute. Turn RIGHT along the lane past The Greyhound Inn, dating from the 16thC, and a large walled garden. *Beyond is the former 18thC manor house, replaced by Shotwick House, now Shotwick Park, in 1872. This lane is possibly part of an ancient road which led to Shotwick castle.* At the entrance to Shotwick Park go along a narrow fenced path alongside the driveway to a kissing gate. Follow the waymarked permissive path across the field to another kissing gate onto a cross path. Follow it LEFT by a small wooded dingle, shortly entering Bluebell Wood, to reach a path T-junction at the wooded edge of the old cliffs.

**2** Turn RIGHT down to cross a large footbridge. The path rises then continues through the wood via another large footbridge. At the wood edge the path bends to a kissing gate, then continues alongside the fence past the site of Shotwick Castle to another kissing gate and information board. Follow the path up the edge of two fields. In the field corner, where there are two kissing gates, turn RIGHT along the field edge, through a kissing gate and another ahead. Go up and along the field edge to a kissing gate, then down the next field to cross a stiled footbridge. Continue across the field, through a narrow strip of woodland via two kissing gates, then across another field to a kissing gate to reach the village road beyond. Turn LEFT back to the start.

# SAUGHALL

**DESCRIPTION** A 5 mile walk exploring the countryside near Saughall, featuring attractive woodland of Shotwick Park, a section of the Chester to Connah's Quay railway path and an ancient highway. Allow about 3 hours.

**START** Church Way, Saughall [SJ 363704].

**DIRECTIONS** See Walk 10.

**I** Follow instructions in paragraph **1** of **Walk 10**.

**2** Turn LEFT and follow the path through the trees and down to a stile. Turn LEFT along a wide path then go through a kissing gate on the right. Go across the field, soon near a stream, to cross a stile, footbridge and a stile beyond. Turn RIGHT to a stile/gate. Turn LEFT and follow the high hedge to a gate, then go along the edge of the next large field to another gate. Continue ahead to a kissing gate onto the end of Green Lane. Turn LEFT past Barleywood and continue briefly along the rough lane, then turn RIGHT past barriers to join the Chester to Connah's Quay railway path shared with National Cycle route 5. *Opened in 1890, the former Mickle*

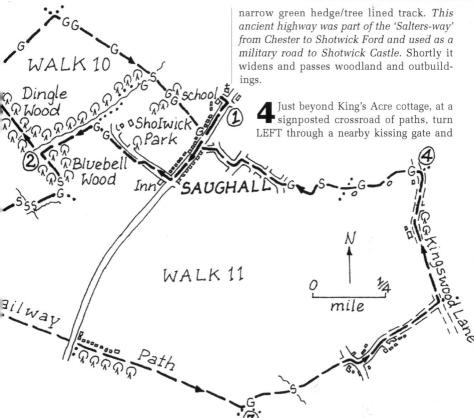

narrow green hedge/tree lined track. *This ancient highway was part of the 'Salters-way' from Chester to Shotwick Ford and used as a military road to Shotwick Castle.* Shortly it widens and passes woodland and outbuildings.

**4** Just beyond King's Acre cottage, at a signposted crossroad of paths, turn LEFT through a nearby kissing gate and

*Trafford to Dee Marsh railway closed to passengers in 1969 and to freight in 1992. It served the former John Summers steel works at Shotton, and carried steel, coal, minerals, agricultural products. It is now a popular 'greenway'.* Follow it LEFT towards Chester, passing under a nearby bridge and later another by a small housing estate.

**3** At a second set of gates across the former railway line, turn LEFT to a nearby stiled gate. Go along the field edge to a stile/boundary gap, then angle RIGHT across the next field to a stile/gate. Follow the farm track up onto the former low cliffs, along the field edge, then between hedges to a road. Cross to the pavement opposite and follow it RIGHT, then turn LEFT along Green Lane to Poplars Farm. Continue along the track past outbuildings and on to reach a junction with Kingswood Lane. Turn LEFT along the

**③** go along a narrow enclosed path. At the fence corner follow the path LEFT alongside the fence past a small pond, then RIGHT near the hedge boundary to a footbridge in the field corner and a kissing gate beyond. Keep ahead across the field past a small reedy pond to go through a waymarked gap in the hedge ahead to a signposted crossroad of paths. Continue ahead across the field to a footbridge and stile in the hedge. Turn LEFT and follow the next field edge round to a kissing gate in the far corner. Follow the short enclosed path between houses to a nearby road (The Ridings) at the edge of Saughall. Follow it RIGHT through the housing estate. At the junction turn LEFT, then RIGHT along Darlington Crescent. As it bends right go along Smithy Close on the left. At its end pass through barriers to reach the nearby main road in Saughall. Turn RIGHT back to the start.

## WALK 12

# SHOTWICK

**DESCRIPTION** A 6¼ mile walk (**A**) exploring the countryside between historic Shotwick village and Saughall. From Shotwick's 12thC church the route follows an ancient highway, crosses a road intersection, then continues to Saughall, en route crossing the former low cliffs of the Dee. After passing through the village, with its 16thC Greyhound Inn (check opening times), the walk returns via ancient Shotwick Park estate, featuring attractive woodland and Shotwick Castle, then field paths and quiet lanes. Allow about 3½ hours. A shorter 5 mile walk (**B**), omitting Saughall, is included. See *Walk 10 for information on Saughall and Shotwick Park.*
**START** Shotwick [SJ 337718] or Saughall [SJ 363704].
**DIRECTIONS** Shotwick is signposted from the A550. See Walk 10 for the Saughall start.

*S**hotwick** lies at the end of an ancient ford across the Dee to North Wales. It was in use until the 18thC. It was an important trading route since before Norman times, and by the Middle Ages a well-established 'Saltesway' for the carrying of Cheshire salt. Despite the hazards of shifting sands, this tidal crossing was for many travellers preferable to other longer land journeys prone to highwaymen. Several armies crossed the ford: in 1245 under Henry III and in 1278 and 1284 under Edward I in campaigns against the Welsh. 14thC records indicate a ferryboat also operated here.*

*For a period during the 15th/16thC, when large ships were unable to reach Chester, Shotwick was the main Dee port, providing a deep tidal anchorage for ships to offload their cargoes. At that time the tidal waters lapped the churchyard walls of 12thC St Michael's. The porch stonework has deep groves made by archers sharpening their arrows. The village buildings are mainly 17thC and include the former Greyhound Inn.*

**1** After visiting the church go through the small Marsh access gate by the churchyard wall and follow the initially narrow track for ½ mile to join Green Lane West. Follow it under the large road bridge. At a T-junction by Deeside Industrial estate cross to the pavement opposite and follow it LEFT, then continue along Drome Road, past a large roundabout. Cross the slip road then the bridge over the busy A494 road. Cross the next slip road and follow the pavement LEFT, soon bending RIGHT along Green Lane East. Continue to a crossing point just before a bus shelter. Turn LEFT along the pavement opposite, then go along the no through road (Green Lane East), signposted to MOD Sealand. Just before the entrance to DSG cross the road to join a wide tarmaced cycle/walkway, soon parallel with the nearby slip road.

**2** Shortly, go through a kissing gate on the right then follow a stiled path along the edge of a series of fields to eventually reach the end of a grassy Scots pine covered embankment. *You are walking where the Dee once flowed, on land reclaimed after the New Cut. The wooded boundary further to your left is the old coastline.* Turn LEFT over a stile ahead, then a large footbridge and a stile beyond. Go across the field, initially near a stream, to a kissing gate/gate. (For **Walk B** turn left to a nearby stile and follow a path up and along the wooded former cliffs to point **5**.)

**3** Turn RIGHT along the wide path, then go through a small gate on the left. Follow the path up through the tree covered slope of the former cliffs to a kissing gate. The path continues across the field towards Saughall to a footbridge in the hedge, then across the next field to a kissing gate. Follow the hedge-lined path to another kissing gate into Saughall. Turn LEFT along Seahill Road past The Greyhound Inn and continue along Church Road through the village.

**4** About 20 yards beyond Saughall Service Station take a signposted path between Rustic Cottage and Woodside House to a kissing gate. Follow the path across the field to pass through a narrow strip of woodland via two kissing gates. Continue across the next field to cross a stiled footbridge. Turn LEFT

to a footbridge and a stile beyond. Go along the next field edge past a stile and on to cross two stiles in the corner. Go along the next field edge to a stile by water troughs, cross a farm track, then a stile/footbridge on the right. Continue along the large field edge to a kissing gate and another beyond.

**6** Turn RIGHT up the gated track, on a recreational route signposted to Shotwick/ Parkgate, to reach the driveway leading to Pleasant View Farm. Turn RIGHT up the

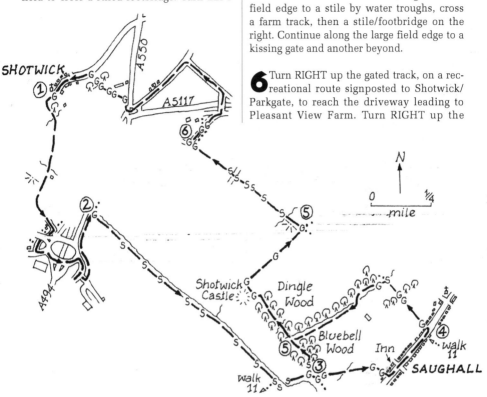

on the waymarked permissive path to a nearby kissing gate. Follow the path through the edge of woodland, across a footbridge over the stream then between a field and a narrow wooded dingle to enter Bluebell Wood.

**5** At a path T-junction at the wooded edge of former cliffs, turn RIGHT down to cross a large footbridge. The path rises then continues through the wood via another large footbridge. At the wood edge the path bends to a kissing gate, then continues alongside the fence past the site of Shotwick Castle to another kissing gate and an information board. Continue up the edge of two fields. Just before the corner go through a kissing gate on the left. Go along the field edge down

road and follow it across the nearby bridge over the busy A5117. At the junction with Bypass Road keep ahead. At the T-junction turn LEFT, soon passing Grange Farm. Just after the road bends right follow the designated cycle/walkway to cross the nearby A550 by the Pegasus traffic light controlled crossing. At the far side turn RIGHT, then LEFT through a gap in the embankment, signposted to Shotwick, to a kissing gate. Go down the field to a small gate in the right hand corner and a kissing gate beyond. Descend the next field edge to cross a gated footbridge. Go up the field to a partly hidden kissing gate in the tree boundary onto the road below. Follow it into nearby Shotwick.

## WALK 13

# OLD QUAY

**DESCRIPTION** A 2¼ mile walk to the site of a 16thC estuary port, returning via field paths and the Wirral Way. Allow about 1½ hours.

**START** Wirral Country Park car park, Parkgate [SJ 284779] or South Parade by the Old Quay pub, Parkgate [SJ 281778].

**DIRECTIONS** Follow the B5139 from Neston. At Parkgate, just after it bends left towards the estuary, the entrance to the Wirral Country Park car park is on the left.

**1** From the car park return to the road and follow it LEFT past the cricket ground. On the bend by the Old Quay pub turn LEFT along South Parade to its end by Far End cottage. Follow a path across sandstone blocks and beside the sea wall, then bending away from the estuary to reach a road. Follow it RIGHT past other houses. At its end, go along a short enclosed path, then continue along Manorial Road South. On the bend, turn RIGHT on a signposted path (Old Quay ½ mile) to reach the edge of the marsh. Follow the path southwards along its rush covered edge to a kissing gate, then along a field edge and through a gap in the hedge boundary corner. Continue ahead to cross a footbridge over a stream – *with the remains of the old sea wall to your right* – and on to reach a sandstone stile at Old Quay. *In the 1540s a stone pier was built here, some 10 miles down river from Chester, to serve as its 'out port', when navigation to the city by large ships was becoming difficult. From a good anchorage nearby, goods were landed on the quay and taken by small boats to Chester. It was known as 'New Key' and was in regular use until early 18thC, when it was replaced by the new port at Parkgate. After its decline it became known as 'Old Quay'. Adjoining the quay was Key House, a prominent landmark and at one time a prison.*

**2** Turn LEFT and follow the wide stony path through two kissing gates and over a footbridge, After the stony path bends left go through a kissing gate on the right and follow a path directly ahead to pass through the tree boundary – *marking the former branch railway line which served the nearby Neston colliery.* Go along the next field edge to a kissing gate to join the Wirral Way. Turn LEFT and follow the wide stony path back to the start.

## WALK 14

# DENHAM QUAY

**DESCRIPTION** A 5½ mile walk featuring two historic former estuary ports, one with a substantial quay remaining, an old inn used by miners at a nearby colliery, delightful bridleways and an attractive section of the Wirral Way to finish. Allow about 3 hours.

**START** As Walk 13.

**1** Follow instructions in paragraph **1** of **Walk 13**.

**2** Cross the stile and follow the path along the edge of the saltmarsh, then a track past the reclaimed spoil heaps of the former Little Neston/Wirral Colliery to a road end at Little Neston and an information board. *From the mid 18thC until the mine's closure in 1927, coal was extracted from a network of tunnels running two miles under the estuary. For many years it was transported along two underground canals built about 1791 in small boats, by men pushing against the roof. During the 18th and 19thC coal was shipped by boat to North Wales, Ireland and the Isle of Man, but by 1855 coalmining had ceased due to silting of the river. The arrival of the railway enabled mining to restart and at its peak in the early 1920s over 300 workers were employed.* Continue ahead along the rough road to reach The Harp Inn. *It was built for miners, many of whom came from Staffordshire, and is now popular with wildfowlers returning from shooting on the marshes.* Continue along the road to another information board. A path through the trees leads to the nearby large red sandstone blocks of Denhall Quay. *It was a popular anchorage during the 15thC and 16thC, and was still in use at the end of the 17thC when*

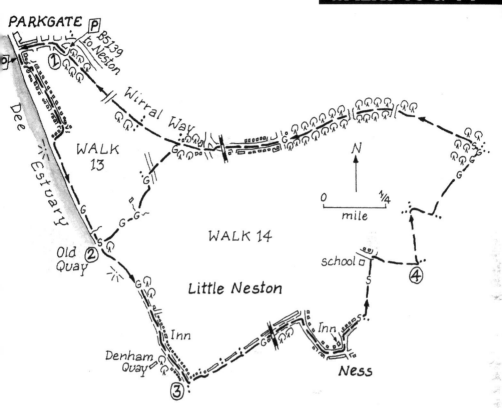

ten ships and 55 men were registered here. *Unlike the Old Quay, it remained navigable after the New Cut in 1737, and was then used to export coal and import limestone and slate until silting finally prevented barges reaching the quay.* Continue along the road through a small residential area. It soon narrows and becomes a stony path.

**3** At a finger post turn LEFT and follow a tarmaced path past dwellings, then between a housing estate and fields. Later, continue along a narrow stony path past further houses to a kissing gate, then follow a track under the railway line and up to a minor road. Follow it RIGHT. Just before crossroads, take a tarmaced path angling LEFT up past a seat and bus shelter. *Nearby is The Wheatcheaf pub.* Cross to the pavement opposite and follow it LEFT, then go along Cumbers Lane. Continue along a path past Cumbers Cottages into a field. Keep

ahead with the main path, soon bending LEFT across the large field to a stile and on past a children's play area to a road. Turn RIGHT and go along a signposted tree, then hedge-lined bridleway (Woodfall Lane).

**4** Shortly, turn LEFT along a delightful narrow tree-lined path, then turn RIGHT along a wide hedge-lined bridleway. It soon bends LEFT and continues through gates. Just before an old railway bridge cross a stile on the left and follow a path up onto the former embanked railway line to join the Wirral Way. Follow it under a road bridge, through an impressive mature tree-lined sandstone cutting, under another tall bridge and on to Mellock Lane/Bushell Road. Go along Station Road opposite to its end, then pass under the railway bridge. Just beyond a car park you rejoin the tree-lined Wirral Way, which crosses a road then continues back to the start.

# PARKGATE

**DESCRIPTION** A 4 mile walk around Parkgate, providing an insight into the area's important maritime past. After following a delightful section of the Wirral Way to Cottage Lane, the route descends to a once important crossing point of the Dee estuary. It then follows the old sea wall along the edge of Parkgate Marsh and Gayton Sands RSPB Nature Reserve, before continuing along Parkgate's historic seafront. Allow about 2½ hours. Shorter route options are shown.

**START** Wirral Country Park car park, Parkgate [SJ 284779] or Old Baths car park, Parkgate [SJ 274790].

**DIRECTIONS** Follow the B5139 from Neston. At Parkgate, just after it bends left towards the estuary, the entrance to the car park is on the left. The alternative Old Baths car park is reached from the bend of the road by The Boathouse at the northern end of Parkgate.

*The attractive largely 18thC frontage of Parkgate is a reminder of its former prestigious past. It began as a village on land previously used as a deer park, then in the 18thC became as a major passenger port for Ireland and fashionable seaside resort. Ships anchored in the main channel of the river, originally 50 yards from the seawall.*

*Famous travellers included the composer Handel, heading for the first performance of 'The Messiah' in Dublin in 1741, and John Wesley, the preacher, who made numerous crossings. Turner painted here, and visitors included Mrs Fitzherbert, who subsequently married the Prince of Wales, later George IV, and in 1784 Emma Hart, later Lady Hamilton, mistress of Admiral Lord Nelson.*

*By 1815, the Dee no longer flowed along the Wirral shore, ending the Parkgate-Dublin service. Parkgate then became a fishing village famous for its shrimps, and a well-known bathing resort until the 1930s, when the water reached the seawall only on exceptionally high tides. It remains popular with visitors today and is now known for its homemade ice cream.*

**1** Go to a nearby concrete pill-box and descend steps to a kissing gate. Cross the road and turn RIGHT past a railway wagon display, then just before the bend, turn LEFT onto the Wirral Way. Follow the wide tree-lined former Hooton-West Kirby branch railway line, briefly shared with National Cycle route 56, to cross a bridge near a school. Later, it passes under Boathouse Lane and Backwood Hall bridges, then between sections of a golf course crossed by a footpath. At the next bridge take a signposted path on the right up to Cottage Lane.

**2** Follow the road LEFT down to its end by Gayton Cottage at the edge of the expansive area of marsh. *It is hard to imagine that this was once the high water mark of the Dee, providing an anchorage for ships in the Middle Ages, and used as a crossing point by Edward I in 1277 to Flint after a stay at Shotwick Castle. In the early 19thC a regular sailing boat ferry service operated between here and Greenfield on the Welsh coast. Gayton Cottage, the former ferry house, could accommodate up to 20 travellers.* Follow the path south along the top of the red sandstone former sea-wall towards Parkgate. *The retreat of the tidal waters has left a vast area of mudflats, sandflats and saltmarsh that now form Parkgate Marsh and Gayton Sands RSPB Nature Reserve. These habitats provide rich feeding and safe roosting areas for one of the largest wintering areas of ducks and wading birds in the British Isles.* Eventually you reach the Old Baths car park – *built on the site of the former popular sea water baths (1923 – 45).*

**3** Follow the roadside path to the main road by The Boathouse. *At the beginning of the 18thC, an anchorage known as the Beer House Hole had developed just offshore from here. A popular ferry also operated across the Dee to Flint. At first it carried only passengers, but by the late 18thC also horses and other animals. Later a landing-stage was built at the Ferry House Inn, as it was then known, to remove the indignity of ladies being carried into the boats! The ferry ceased about 1860. A short-lived steam packet service to Bagillt began in 1817.* Continue by

Gayton

golf course

Backwood Hall

WALK 15

Wirral

WALK 16 Way

Old sea wall

Nature Reserve

Dee Estuary

The Boathouse

PARKGATE

Cowfield school

The Ropeway

school

## WALK 16

# BACKWOOD HALL

**DESCRIPTION** A 4 mile walk, with a shorter route option, featuring an elevated outward route via 19thC Backwood Hall, offering extensive estuary views, and a return along the Wirral Way. Allow about 2½ hours.
**START** Wirral Country Park car park, Parkgate [SJ 284779].
**DIRECTIONS** See Walk 15.

surfaced walkway, shared with Cycle Route 56, past 'The Cowfield' – *a large green space being managed for community use.* Turn LEFT along a lane, then at the junction with Brook Lane, continue ahead along a wide rough stony lane. At Brookhouse Lane follow a signposted path along the access lane opposite to pass Backwood Mews and nearby Backwood Hall.

**2** At the track junction keep ahead to a waymarked gate. Go down the path to a gate/footbridge/gate, then up the field to a hidden small wooden gate. Follow the waymarked path along the top edge of the golf course, then through trees and past a finger post marking a short cut path across the golf course. Soon, you join a rough track, which passes houses and becomes cobbled. At a road junction turn LEFT down Cottage Lane, past the entrance to Heswall Golf Club and houses. Shortly take a wide path on the left down to join the Wirral Way. Follow it southwards for 1¾ miles to the bend of the road near the start.

the old sea wall through Parkgate along The Parade, built as a promenade in the 1840s for visitors. After passing Mostyn House School – *formerly the 18thC George Inn* – follow the road left back to the start.

## WALK 16

**I** Go to a nearby concrete pill-box and descend steps to a kissing gate onto the road. Go along The Ropeway opposite, soon continuing as a wide enclosed path between houses, then past a green to Brooklyn Road. *The Ropeway was originally created for visitors to use when the weather was too bad for strolling along the Parade.* Follow it RIGHT up to Parkgate primary school. Pass under the former railway bridge and follow the wide

From the pool by the Visitor Centre head down towards the estuary, then turn LEFT along the cliffs past seats, keeping away from the edge. At a wooden fence corner beyond the last seat you have a choice. (For **Walk B** continue along the cliff top to Tinkers Bell etc as previously described.) For **Walk A** turn LEFT along the wide path, then follow an enclosed path bending RIGHT and passing round a reedy pool. Go past another pool, then through a gap by a gate ahead onto the Wirral Way. Turn RIGHT. At a finger post turn LEFT (Wirral Circular Trail) to join the nearby former railway line heading south eastwards. After passing under Dungeon Bridge, it continues past a signposted path to The Dungeon (your return route).

# HESWALL FIELDS & DALES

**DESCRIPTION** A varied 5 mile walk (**A**) featuring cliff top views, wildlife pools, a section of the Wirral Way, Heswall Fields owned by the National Trust, Heswall Dales Local Nature Reserve, and The Dungeon, a delightful wooded gorge. Allow about 3 hours. An alternative outward route, avoiding high tide, making a 4½ mile walk (**B**), is to descend the cliffs via a stepped path at Tinkers Bell and follow the beach/foreshore to Sheldrake's restaurant by an area of small boats, then go up Banks Road to join Walk A at point 3. Here you can also return directly along the Wirral Way, making an alternative 3½ mile walk. *The Visitor Centre is open daily all year. See Walk 19 for information on the Country Park and former railway.*

**START** Thurstaston Visitor Centre [SJ 238834].

**DIRECTIONS** See Walk 19.

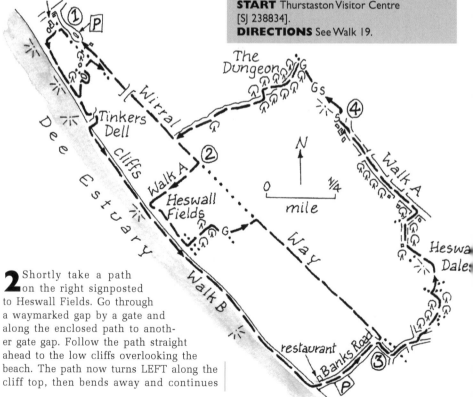

**2** Shortly take a path on the right signposted to Heswall Fields. Go through a waymarked gap by a gate and along the enclosed path to another gate gap. Follow the path straight ahead to the low cliffs overlooking the beach. The path now turns LEFT along the cliff top, then bends away and continues near the field edge, soon passing cliff top seats. At the last seat before the field corner (where there is access to the beach if you wish to join Walk B) turn LEFT to go through a waymarked gap by a gate and one beyond. Go along the enclosed path then bear RIGHT across the narrow field to a kissing gate opposite. Follow the narrow hedge-lined path to leave Heswall Fields and rejoin the wide walkers section of the Wirral Way. Follow it RIGHT. After ½ mile just before a bridge, turn RIGHT signposted to nearby Banks Road. Turn LEFT.

**3** Follow the road up and across Delavor Road Bridge and continue along its left-hand side. Shortly, cross Pipers Lane, then take the tarmaced path angling across to join Bush Way. Soon take a path into Heswall Dales Local Nature Reserve. After a gap in the fence at a crossroad of paths, turn LEFT. Follow the path up through trees and past a cross-path in a more open area. Continue up the path, soon bending LEFT at a waymarked path junction to cross the bracken, gorse, heather and birch covered hillside to eventually reach an access track near Dale Cottage. Go up the narrow stony track to Oldfield Road and follow it LEFT to a junction with Oldfield Drive. Continue along the track ahead on the signposted path to Thurstaston, soon passing Oldfield Farm. Follow the path past the last outbuilding to a sandstone stile by a bench seat at a good viewpoint.

**4** Follow the enclosed path between fields to a stile and a kissing gate beyond. Continue on the enclosed path to go through another kissing gate into the top of Dungeon Wood. Turn LEFT and follow the path through trees by the stream, shortly crossing to the opposite bank and passing above the deep gorge before descending to a waymarker post. Bend LEFT down the stepped path to cross the stream, then turn RIGHT. Now follow the enclosed path by the stream past fields to rejoin the Wirral Way. Later, go past the gate ahead and follow the track to the car park.

## WALK 18
# THURSTASTON BEACH

**DESCRIPTION** A 2¼ mile (**A**) or 1½ mile walk (**B**) featuring a small Nature Reserve, a fine stretch of beach at low tide, cliffs and good estuary views. Allow about 1½ hours.
**START** Thurstaston Visitor Centre [SJ 238834].
**DIRECTIONS** See Walk 19.

**I** From the former railway platform follow the Wirral Way north under Station Road bridge. After about ½ mile turn LEFT through a gap signposted to Dawpool Nature Reserve. Go through a gap adjoining a gate just before a road into the Reserve. Go along the path, then when it splits, bend LEFT past a bench seat. At a path T-junction turn RIGHT, then at the next LEFT down to seats overlooking the estuary onto the road below. Follow it RIGHT past a car park to the Dee Sailing Club. Descend the slipway then walk along the shore beneath the red sandstone cliffs, shortly passing Shore Cottage. (For **Walk B**, just beyond take a stepped path up through trees onto the cliffs and continue to the end of Station Road. Go through a gap on the right into Wirral Country Park and return to the pool by the Visitor Centre.)

**2** Continue along the beach, then take a formal stepped path up onto the cliffs and cross a stream at Tinkers Dell. Continue along the cliffs, keeping away from the edge, soon passing seats, then head across open ground to the pool by the Visitor Centre.

*Sailing Club*
*Dawpool Nature Reserve*
*Wirral Way*
*Thurstaston beach*
*Visitor Centre*
*N*
*0   ¼ mile*
*Tinkers Dell*

# THURSTASTON & CALDY HILLS

**DESCRIPTION** A 6½ mile walk exploring the attractive varied countryside between Thurstaston and West Kirby, featuring two low hilltops offering extensive views, and attractive woodland. The route passes through Thurstaston, then Thurstaston Common, an area of heath, woodland and sandstone outcrops, now a Local Nature Reserve owned by the National Trust. It then visits Stapledon Wood and Caldy Hill, an attractive area of lowland heath and mixed woodland, featuring a 19thC maritime beacon. It then returns along the Wirral Way via Cubbins Green overlooking the estuary. Allow about 4 hours.

**START** Thurstaston Visitor Centre car park [SJ 239835]. Alternative starts from other car parks are shown.

**DIRECTION** The Wirral Country Park Visitor Centre lies near the estuary just before the end of Station Road, accessed from the roundabout on the A540 near the Cottage Loaf pub.

*The Wirral Way Country Park is based on the former Hooton to West Kirby railway. It was first opened from Hooton to Parkgate in 1866, then extended in 1886 to West Kirby, with links to Birkenhead. At its peak the line had twelve passenger trains daily in each direction, with early morning trains carrying commuters to Woodside Ferry for the crossing to Liverpool, and day excursions bringing people to the seaside and Parkgate. Freight trains primarily carried coal from Neston, but also fish, shrimps and prawns from Parkgate, as well as milk and livestock from local farms. The line finally closed in 1962 and was then opened in 1973 as Britain's first country park. Thurstaston Visitor Centre, on the site of the former station, is open daily all year and houses interesting displays and exhibitions. Just offshore was a deep water anchorage known as Dawpool/Redbank, which was in use between the 14th and 19thC.*

**1** Return to Station Road and walk along the pavement up to Thurstaston – *an attractive ancient village centred around St Bartholomew's church and Thurstaston Hall* – then continue up to the A540 roundabout. Turn LEFT and immediately cross to the pavement opposite and follow it past the Cottage Loaf pub. Shortly, go through a kissing gate into Thurstaston Common and follow the path through trees and on past Dawpool school. Just beyond the Old School House turn sharp LEFT up a wide sandstone path through trees, soon bending RIGHT onto the top of Thurstaston Hill. Go past a trig point and a commemorative stone pillar then continue with the wide sandy path along the edge of the sandstone escarpment past seats. After a gentle descent the sandstone path narrows, passes through an area of gorse and birch, with the rugby pitch below. Continue with the main path through trees. After a brief open section the path descends through trees then levels out. Keep ahead on the main woodland path to reach a National Trust sign just before a wall gap ahead.

**2** Turn LEFT between the wall and iron railings to a kissing gate and on to reach a road. Go along a track opposite, through a kissing gate at the entrance to Frankby cottage, and along an enclosed path to the A540. Go along the pavement opposite to enter the suburbs of West Kirby. After passing Grange Cross Lane the road rises. When it levels out turn LEFT into Kings Drive North to enter Stapledon Wood. Keep ahead, then follow the waymarked bridleway through the attractive woodland. At a lane do a sharp U-turn RIGHT to follow a path through the trees. Go up its left fork and past a wooden fence corner by a tennis court. Continue with the main woodland path to a wall gap into a wide walled bridleway. Turn RIGHT, then LEFT through another wall gap and follow a path through rhododendrons, past side paths, to enter an open section of heather, gorse and small trees. *You are now on Caldy Hill, an important habitat for a variety of reptiles and birds.*

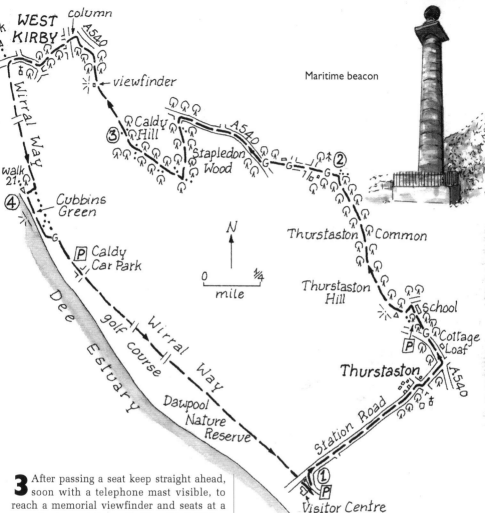

Maritime beacon

**3** After passing a seat keep straight ahead, soon with a telephone mast visible, to reach a memorial viewfinder and seats at a superb viewpoint overlooking West Kirby. Continue with the main path, past a wall and side paths to reach a large inscribed sandstone column near the A540 – *erected in 1841 as a beacon for mariners*. From a seat take a stepped path down to a road. Go down the enclosed path opposite between houses and through mature woodland to another road. Follow it RIGHT past Carpenters Lane and St Bridget's Church in the shady suburbs of West Kirby. Just before the bridge go down steps on the left to join the Wirral Way. Turn LEFT along the former railway line, soon passing under a road bridge. After another ⅓ mile, go down a path on the right after a small wood to enter Cubbins Green. Follow a path ahead to its edge above the beach.

**4** Turn LEFT along the grass shelf – *enjoying extensive views across the estuary to the Welsh hills*. At the last seat, follow the path leading away from the estuary to rejoin the Wirral Way. Follow the wide path to Caldy car park, then its access lane to a road. Continue on the Wirral Way for a further 1¼ miles back to the start.

# ROYDEN PARK & THURSTASTON COMMON

**DESCRIPTION** A 2¾ mile (**A**) or 1¾ mile (**B**) walk exploring a popular Local Nature Reserve comprising attractive woodland, heathland, birch scrub and open parkland. The initially shared route passes round the edge of Frankby Mere, a small seasonal tree surrounded lake, before passing the mock-Tudor house of Hillbark. It then leaves Royden Park and heads south across Thurstaston Common to a large sandstone outcrop, known as Thors stone. Walk B now makes a direct return whilst Walk A continues to the extensive viewpoint on Thurstaston Hill, then follows a choice of routes across the eastern side of the Common, before returning to the Park via Roodee Mere. Allow about 2 hours for the main walk.

**START** Royden Park Visitor Centre [SJ 246858] or Thurstaston Common car park [SJ 246846].

**DIRECTIONS** Royden Park is signposted along the B5140 from a roundabout on the A540. The alternative car park adjoins the A540 a short distance from the Cottage Loaf pub and the turning for Thurstaston. (From a gap at the far end of the car park follow a path through trees, then a cross-path left to pass a school to join the main walk at the end of School Lane – point 4.)

*The 250 acres of Royden Park and adjoining Thurstaston Common have been enjoyed by the public for many years for informal recreation. Ownership of the area is divided between Wirral Borough Council and the National Trust, but managed by the Council's Ranger Service. The area provides important habitats for a wide range of wildlife.*

*Royden Park was first developed by Septimus Ledward who built the original Hillbark here in 1870, but it takes its name from a later owner, Sir Ernest B Royden. He*

*arranged for the current house, which was built elsewhere in 1891 to be moved and re-erected in its present location in 1931.*

**1** From the toilets and Visitor Centre/café entrance follow the road back to the main driveway. Keep ahead signposted to Frankby Mere past a small car parking area in the trees. After a gate continue along the old track, then at a gate on the right turn LEFT to follow a path through rhododendrons. At a Frankby Mere Hide sign turn RIGHT and follow the path alongside the wooden fence through more rhododendrons. At the fence corner keep ahead, soon bending half-LEFT past a tree-topped sandstone block, then turn LEFT across the raised causeway. Follow the path through the trees, then just past old iron railings turn RIGHT along another path. Keep with its left fork, soon passing in front of Hillbark. Towards the end of the clearing head to a nearby iron seat on the right.

**2** With your back to its front angle LEFT across a nearby wide path to follow a narrower one to a gap in the wall into National Trust land. Go over a crosspath, and follow a path angling slightly LEFT through trees and across an open area of common, past a small stone inscribed BC. At a path junction keep ahead, soon passing through mature trees and over a crosspath to another BC stone. The path briefly rises across sandstone, then continues through heather/gorse/bracken to another small stone at a crossroad of paths. Keep ahead to pass the end of a wall to a small No. 5 inscribed stone beyond. Continue along the level path through trees parallel with the nearby wall. At a lift stile in the wall angle RIGHT to follow a path to nearby Thors Stone. (For **Walk B** return to the lift stile and follow a path beyond leading left to a wide stony path. Follow it to a kissing gate/gate and just beyond take the left fork through trees. The wide stony path then crosses an open area, before continuing through woodland. Just beyond an information board and the end of a wall turn right, then left along the edge of the large event field to the car park.)

30

**3** Pass round the far end of Thors stone, then take a wide path leading RIGHT through trees up to emerge onto the western sandstone escarpment – *offering extensive views across the Dee estuary to the Welsh coast and hills.* Follow it LEFT up past seats, then a commemorative stone pillar and trig point on Thurstaston Hill. Soon take a path bending LEFT down to the end of School Lane. (Or for the alternative start take a sandstone path descending right.)

**4** Go through a nearby kissing gate and keep ahead on the main path through attractive woodland to reach a stony access track. Here you have a choice of routes. (For **route b** follow the track past Benty Farm, then a wide stony path to a kissing gate/gate into trees. Just beyond take the right fork to another kissing gate/gate, then follow the wide path through trees to a kissing gate and on to a cross-path. Turn left and resume instructions in paragraph **5.**) For **route a** turn RIGHT along the track. Soon turn LEFT along a waymarked path to a nearby lift stile. Follow the path straight ahead along the edge of a clearing and on through trees to a kissing gate onto a cross-path. Follow it LEFT along the edge of the wood, later being joined by route b.

**5** Continue along the edge of the wood. At its corner turn LEFT and follow the path near the perimeter wall. Shortly, bear RIGHT past the end of the wall and follow the path through mixed woodland, then past the miniature railway. Continue past the lily-covered Roodee Mere, then cross the miniature railway line to join a lane which takes you past the Rangers Office and the entrance to the Walled Nature Garden back to the start.

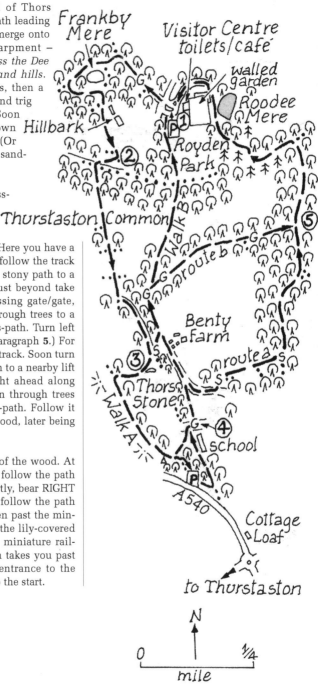

# HILBRE POINT

**DESCRIPTION** A 6 mile mile walk linking West Kirby and Hoylake, offering excellent coastal views. The route first heads south, either along the promenade, or the popular Marine Lake walkway, weather and tide permitting. After visiting Cubbins Green, a delightful grass shelf above the beach, the route follows the Wirral Way north to its end in the centre of West Kirby. It continues to Hoylake and Hilbre Point at the mouth of the Dee estuary near Hilbre Island, before returning through the sand dunes and reedbeds of Red Rocks Marsh Nature Reserve to West Kirby beach. Allow about 3 hours.

**START** Wirral Sailing Centre/toilets, West Kirby [SJ 210867].

**DIRECTIONS** The Sailing Centre lies at the northern end of South Parade by West Kirby beach and Marine Lake, and near Morrisons.

*W*est Kirby *is one of the oldest settlements on the Wirral, with Viking connections. Although overshadowed by Hoylake as a port, it did have a small fleet in the 16thC, but its trade, which included animal skins, steadily declined. It apparently once had a reputation for wrecking and smuggling. The arrival of the railway in 1867 developed the small fishing and farming community into a prosperous commuting town and seaside resort.*

*The only recommended access point at low tide to Hilbre Island is from West Kirby. The three tidal islands of Little Eye, Middle Eye and Hilbre are designated a Local Nature Reserve. Hilbre Island has been occupied since earliest times and monks from Chester Abbey lived here for nearly 400 years. It has a Telegraph Station built by the Trustees of Liverpool Docks in 1841 as part of a chain stretching from Holyhead on Anglesey to Liverpool. It was used as an embarkation point by both Elizabeth I and Cromwell for their campaigns in Ireland.*

**1** Walk south along the promenade past the Marine Lake. Alternatively, just beyond the boat compound turn RIGHT along a road, then go along the edge of a car park to join a wide raised pathway. Follow it around the edge of Marine Lake above the shore, then go along a short road to the end of South Parade. (A low tide option is to follow the shoreline to take a waymarked stony path angling up onto Cubbins Green.) Follow the pavement on the right hand side of the road to a junction, then continue ahead along Sandy lane. Shortly, turn RIGHT along Macdona Drive. At its end, follow a path into Cubbins Green. Walk along this grass shelf – *enjoying panoramic estuary views* – then at the last seat, follow the path leading away from the estuary to join the Wirral Way.

**2** Follow it LEFT under two road bridges, past Victorian Ashton Park, under a cast iron footbridge and on to its end at the main road in West Kirby. Go along Orrysdale Road opposite. At crossroads keep ahead, soon passing a school. When the road bends right keep ahead to join a designated cycle/walkway running alongside the railway line past the golf course. Mid-way take a signposted path through a kissing gate and across the railway line – heeding the warning sign – then follow the walled path to the A540 in Hoylake. Cross to the pavement opposite and turn RIGHT. Soon go through a kissing gate to join a signed footpath to St Hildeburgh's church. Go along the road, then turn RIGHT on a surfaced path along the edge of famous Royal Liverpool Golf Course. At its end continue ahead on grass past the golf club and houses. Now follow a blue line marked on the grass, soon angling LEFT across the corner of the golf course to join a enclosed path to reach a road by the church. Turn LEFT along this attractive road past large houses to the slipway at Hilbre Point. (Part way a road on the right leads to the nearby shore, where at low tide you have the option of walking along the sand to Hilbre Point.) *In the early 19thC Hoylake consisted of a few fishermen's cottages. However, the desire of prosperous Birkenhead and Liverpool businessmen for summer homes, and the arrival of the railway, led to the*

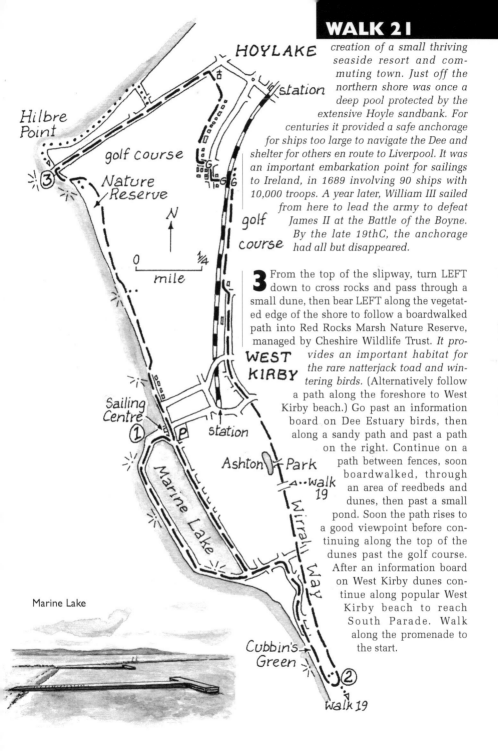

HOYLAKE

Hilbre Point

golf course

Nature Reserve

N

0       ¼
mile

Sailing Centre
①

WEST KIRBY

station

P

Ashton Park

walk 19

Marine Lake

Cubbin's Green

Walk 19

②

③

Marine Lake

creation of a small thriving seaside resort and commuting town. Just off the northern shore was once a deep pool protected by the extensive Hoyle sandbank. For centuries it provided a safe anchorage for ships too large to navigate the Dee and shelter for others en route to Liverpool. It was an important embarkation point for sailings to Ireland, in 1689 involving 90 ships with 10,000 troops. A year later, William III sailed from here to lead the army to defeat James II at the Battle of the Boyne. By the late 19thC, the anchorage had all but disappeared.

**3** From the top of the slipway, turn LEFT down to cross rocks and pass through a small dune, then bear LEFT along the vegetated edge of the shore to follow a boardwalked path into Red Rocks Marsh Nature Reserve, managed by Cheshire Wildlife Trust. *It provides an important habitat for the rare natterjack toad and wintering birds.* (Alternatively follow a path along the foreshore to West Kirby beach.) Go past an information board on Dee Estuary birds, then along a sandy path and past a path on the right. Continue on a path between fences, soon boardwalked, through an area of reedbeds and dunes, then past a small pond. Soon the path rises to a good viewpoint before continuing along the top of the dunes past the golf course. After an information board on West Kirby dunes continue along popular West Kirby beach to reach South Parade. Walk along the promenade to the start.

# FLINT CASTLE & DOCK

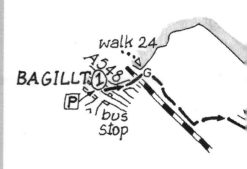

**DESCRIPTION** A meandering 3½ mile walk exploring the edge of the estuary at Flint, featuring its 13thC castle, 19thC port, and a section of the new Wales Coast Path. Allow about 2 hours. It can easily be undertaken as shorter walks.

**START** Flint Castle car park [SJ 246733].

**DIRECTIONS** From the A548 in Flint follow signs for Castle Park industrial estate to find the car park near the estate entrance.

*F**lint Castle (1277-80) was the first castle built by Edward I during his conquest of Wales. It was strategically placed to secure the ancient low tide ford across the Dee from Shotwick, from where Edward led a great army. It features a Great Tower or Donjon of French influence. Nearby he founded a town for English settlers, and granted it a Royal Charter in 1284. The capitulation of Richard II to Henry Bolingbroke, later Henry IV, at Flint Castle in 1399, leading to his abdication, is immortalised in a scene from Shakespeare's Richard II. In 1403, the castle was besieged and the town attacked during Owain Glyndŵr's uprising against the English. During the Civil War, the castle changed hands several times before finally succumbing to the Parliamentarians in 1646, after which it was dismantled.*

*By the early 19thC Flint was a flourishing seaport and a fashionable bathing place which became more popular with the the arrival of the railway. For over a hundred years Flint Dock, a long narrow tidal inlet, was a flourishing port trading in local lead, coal and later chemicals. In the 20thC paperworks, flour-milling, and textile manufacturing, came to the town.*

**I** First visit the castle then follow the surfaced path to the road. Turn LEFT, then shortly follow a path round the edge of a car park to information boards. Go past the end of the nearby lifeboat station, then follow a wide railed promenade along the estuary edge past the rugby and football grounds. At its end go through a squeeze gap by a gate and follow the surfaced path past a viewing area at the saltmarsh edge. At a path junction turn RIGHT and follow the path to a junction with a cycle/walkway. Go ahead past the football pitch then follow a path along the edge of the park to a gate into Marsh Lane. Turn LEFT to a nearby junction. Keep ahead, and also at the next junction to join your outward route. Follow the road past the castle to a junction. Turn RIGHT, then LEFT along the road through the industrial estate to pass the end of Flint Dock. Just before the entrance to Flint recycling centre go along a cycleway on the left, then take a path signposted to Bagillt through birch woodland. After a gate at a signposted path junction turn RIGHT along a hedge-lined path. After a kissing gate keep ahead on the path's right fork to another kissing gate up onto the nearby low cliffs.

**2** Follow the wide surfaced path to a junction, then LEFT through an area of birch trees to Flint Point – *offering good estuary views.* Continue on a track along the western side of the former Flint Dock, then an access road to a junction at the entrance to Flint recycling centre. Turn LEFT, then follow the signposted Coastal Path/Castle Walk past an information board at the end of Flint Dock and along its birch-covered eastern side. The raised path then meanders along the tree covered estuary edge to eventually reach the car park by Flint Castle.

***B**agillt* *is an industrial village and small port that developed during the 18th and 19thC, with lead and coal mines, zinc and chemical works, a brewery and rope-making works. The remains of leadworks and large areas of waste testify to this being the most important lead working area along the estuary. The nearby water gutter, now silted, was an important cargo port handling large amounts of coal, lead, zinc and copper.*

# BAGILLT TO FLINT

**DESCRIPTION** A 3½ mile linear walk on the new Wales Coast Path along the edge of the estuary past the former Flint Dock to 13thC Flint Castle (See Walk 22 for information.) The route finishes at a bus stop near McDonald's on the A548, from where you can catch the regular X11 bus back to Bagillt. Alternatively, use a nearby car park on the corner of Feather Street, and first take the bus to Bagillt.
**START** Car park, Bagillt [SJ 219753].
**DIRECTIONS** The car park lies in the centre of Bagillt near the Stag Inn.

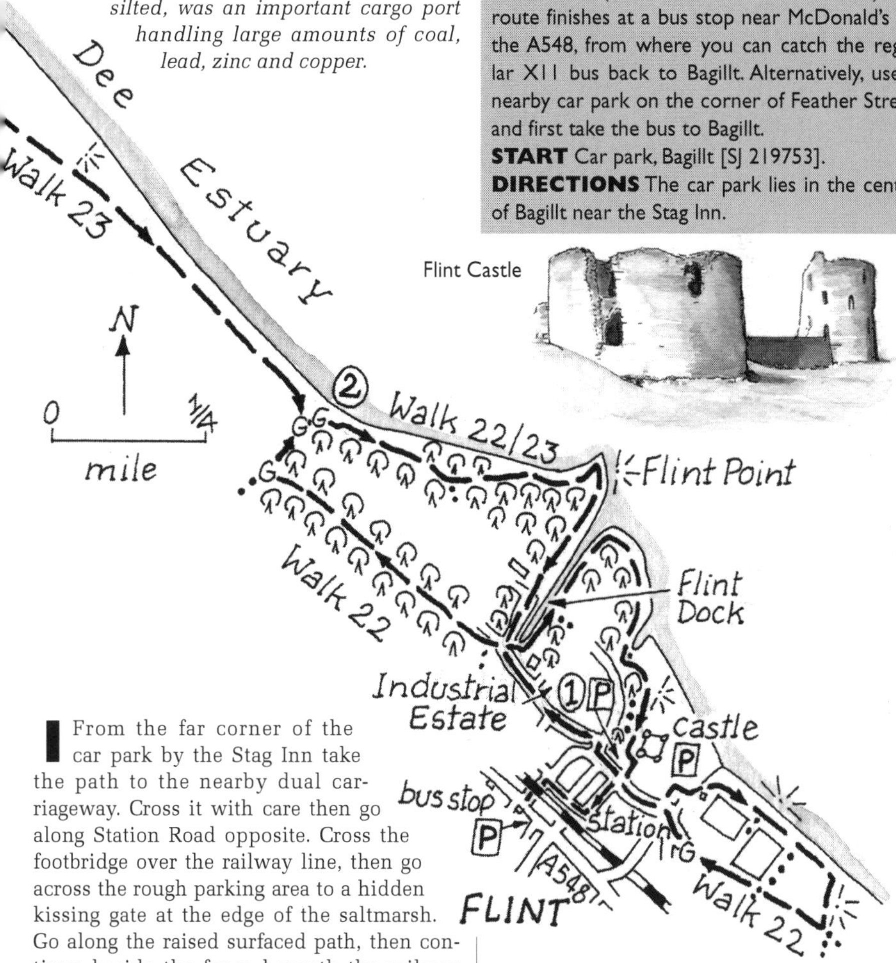

Flint Castle

I From the far corner of the car park by the Stag Inn take the path to the nearby dual carriageway. Cross it with care then go along Station Road opposite. Cross the footbridge over the railway line, then go across the rough parking area to a hidden kissing gate at the edge of the saltmarsh. Go along the raised surfaced path, then continue beside the fence beneath the railway line to the end of the embankment ahead. Now follow a path along the top of the stone clad embankment, gradually becoming closer to the estuary edge. At its end a waymarked path leads towards a kissing gate/gate. Just before them, follow a path LEFT to another kissing gate onto the nearby low cliffs.

2 Follow instructions in paragraph **2** of Walk 22 to Flint Castle car park. After visiting the castle follow the surfaced path to the road. Go along Castle Street ahead, then turn RIGHT along Corporation Street. Pass under the railway bridge to the A548 and a bus stop opposite near McDonalds.

35

*Greenfield Valley, near to sources of lead and other ores, and with easy access by sea to Liverpool, developed rapidly during the 18thC as an important industrial centre, regarded as the cradle of the Industrial Revolution in North Wales. Its constant flow of water – 4,000 gallons a minute – which never* **Greenfield** *froze, provided the power for a line of mills and factories that stretched down the narrow valley. It steadily declined during the 19thC with the development of steam power, and the need for larger sites and better port facilities.*

**I** Go along the High Street and at its end turn RIGHT. Cross the inner ring road and go down steps then Well Street. Continue down past the graveyard to St. James church and St. Winefride's chapel, then down the B5121 to the entrance of St. Winefride's Well (**A**) *(open daily)*. *Enclosed in an early 16thC chapel, the famous well chamber with bath, renowned for its healing properties, has attracted pilgrims for many centuries.* Continue past the Art & Craft Mill/Tea rooms. Just before commercial premises turn RIGHT and follow the signposted path up to a kissing gate, then its waymarked left fork alongside a wall and past seats.

**2** Just before a large finger post, turn LEFT down a stepped path. Turn RIGHT through an iron archway and go along a path, soon alongside Battery Pool. Turn RIGHT across the dam above the site of Greenfield Mills (**B**). *Established in 1776, the Battery Works produced brass pots and pans, which were sent via Liverpool to Africa and exchanged for slaves.* Continue up past a chimney through trees to join the track bed of the former Holywell branch railway *– the steepest passenger railway in Great Britain.* Follow it LEFT down the wooded valley past waymarked side paths. At a staggered junction of paths, turn LEFT down a stepped path, past the nearby dam of a former mill pool and through Meadow Mill site (**C**) *– which made rollers for printing patterns on cloth and copper sheets.* Continue past the large Flour Mill pool then follow a narrow lane past the Lower Cotton Mill (**D**) *– used between 1785-1840 for spinning cotton brought from the Americas –* then the former Abbey Wire Mill (**E**).

**3** When it bends left continue between buildings and past the Farm Museum (F). Just to the west is a mill pool (**G**) *– all that remains of the important Parys Mine Company copper works built in 1787, which produced copper fittings and sheathing for wooden sailing ships.* With a café ahead turn RIGHT past the Visitor Centre and on past Basingwerk Abbey [1132–1536] (**H**), then down to the large car park by the A548. Follow the pavement opposite LEFT, then turn RIGHT along Dock Road. Follow it over the railway line, then past the end of Greenfield Dock – *once a busy port, with up to 40 ships trading in raw materials and finished products from industries in the Greenfield Valley. Short lived ferry services also ran from here in the 19thC.*

**4** Pass under a barrier gate and follow the signposted Bettisfield/Bagillt/Coast Path along the eastern side of the Dock, then across open ground and past an industrial estate. After crossing a narrow creek the gated Coast Path continues on an embankment along the edge of the saltmarsh, then crosses an old industrial site to a kissing gate just before the railway line at the head of Dee Bank Gutter (**J**). *This small port was once linked to nearby leadworks and a foundry. Briefly in the early 19thC passenger services*

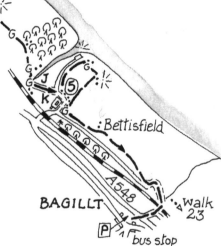

*to Liverpool via Parkgate and Hoylake operated from here. It is known locally as 'The Holy' from the daily average of 23 million gallons of water which gushes from the outlet of the Milwr tunnel, which originally shared the same source as St Winefride's Holy Well. The 10 mile tunnel was driven inland from here in stages between 1897–1957, primarily to drain lead mines in Holywell and Halkyn*

**WALK 24**

# HOLYWELL TO BAGILLT

**DESCRIPTION** A 5¼ mile linear walk, linked to a regular bus service, featuring a newly created section of the Coast Path along the Dee estuary and the area's fascinating industrial and maritime past. The route descends to famous St Winefride's Well, which gave the town its name, then explores Greenfield Valley Heritage Park, containing 12thC Basingwerk Abbey and the remains of 18thC mills, factories and mill pools. From historic Greenfield Dock it follows the Coast Path to the new Bettisfield recreational site, near Bagillt. Allow about 3 hours. From the car park by the Stag Inn in the centre of Bagillt turn left to a bus stop to catch the Arriva 11 bus to Holywell centre

**START** Holywell High Street [SJ 185759].

*Mountain.* Continue along an access road to a barrier gate by the corner of a high fence compound, containing the former winding house of Bettisfield Colliery (1872–1934), now a cars spares site (**K**). Cross to a path opposite beneath a sign welcoming you to 'Bettisfield – Gateway to the Dee'.

**5** Follow it LEFT beside the road to a car park overlooking an inlet containing small fishing boats. The estuary path is currently closed, so go through a kissing gate on the right and up onto the main Bettisfield site to an information board at a great viewpoint along the estuary. Now follow a wide path down to a kissing gate opposite the car spares compound. Just beyond bend LEFT past wooden sculptures, a nearby car park and lane. The waymarked Coast Path continues along the edge of the saltmarsh then follows the lane/stony track to a footbridge over the railway at the former Bagillt Station (1849–1965). *The nearby creek, now silted, was once an important cargo port handling large amounts of coal, lead, zinc and copper.* Cross the footbridge and go along Station Road ahead. Cross the dual carriageway with care and follow a path to the car park.

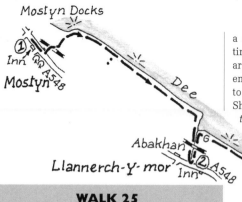

Mostyn Docks

Inn

Mostyn A548

Abakhan

Llannerch-y-mor Inn A548

Dee

Estuary

a footbridge over the railway line and continue to a viewing area overlooking the estuary and across to Mostyn Dock. Follow the embanked track alongside the estuary edge to the entombed Duke of Lancaster or 'Fun Ship' – *the sad legacy of a failed private initiative to create an unusual leisure complex on this former ferry, some years ago.* A path continues alongside the dock's perimeter, then follows its access lane under the low railway bridge to the A548 at Llannerch-y-Mor. (Note that the route past the ship is subject to possible realignment.) *Nearby is Abakhan craft and mill shop, converted from an important 18thC lead-smelting works,* **Greenfield** *whose wheelpit and smelting chimney survive.*

Greenf Dock

Walk 24

Abbey

Inn

## WALK 25

# MOSTYN TO HOLYWELL

**DESCRIPTION** A 5 mile linear walk of great interest from Mostyn to Holywell, linked to a regular bus service. The route follows the Wales Coast Path via Llannerch-y-mor to historic Greenfield Dock, offering close estuary views. It continues to Greenfield Valley Heritage Park (See Walk 24) from where it follows the former steepest conventional passenger railway in Great Britain up to Holywell. Allow about 3 hours. A shorter 3¾ mile walk is to start and finish at either Heritage Par car park shown, taking the bus from opposite the Packet House, Greenfield by the A548/B5121 junction.
**START** The Lletty Inn on the A548, Mostyn [SJ 162803].
**DIRECTIONS** From Holywell take the Arriva bus service 11 to the Lletty Inn.

**2** Follow the signposted path along the stream's eastern bank back under the rail-

Visitor Centre

N

0 ¼ mile

HOLYWELL bus terminus

*M*ostyn Dock, *with its surviving 18thC quay, is the only active large estuary port. During the 19thC, it served a local colliery and Mostyn iron-works. Iron-ore was transported on flat-bottomed boats from ships anchored in mid-river, and the resultant pig iron was shipped to Liverpool. The dock is now involved in the construction and maintenance of nearby windfarms.*

**I** From the Lletty Inn – *dating from 1699 and used as a warehouse, distillery and smuggler's haven* – cross with care to the pavement opposite and follow it RIGHT. Just past a house take a signposted path to cross

way and along the narrow creek leading to the ship, then go along the boulder embanked edge of the estuary to a kissing gate. Continue along the embanked coastal path. *From the mid-18thC embankments were built to help reclaim land from the salt-marsh. After 1½ miles you reach a car park at Greenfield Dock – with an information board overlooking the estuary. It is difficult to imagine that this narrow inlet, now used by small fishing boats, was a busy port in the 18th and 19thC. Up to 40 ships once traded from here in raw materials and finished products from industries in the Greenfield Valley. Nothing remains of the large wharf built in the 18thC. In 1802, a sailing ship ferry service between Greenfield-Parkgate-Chester was established. Between 1857–1865, the iron ship 'Fanny' provided a 1½ hour passenger service to Liverpool. In the 1870s two other similar services were short-lived. Shifting channels in the estuary meant that increasingly only small boats had access to the port, and along with local industries, its importance declined during the 19thC, later losing its rail link.*

**3** Follow nearby Dock Road across the railway line to the A548 in Greenfield. Turn LEFT, then cross the road to follow a signposted path up a narrow road opposite into Greenfield Valley Heritage Park. Turn LEFT past the Visitor Centre and Basingwerk Abbey (1132–1536), then take the path's right fork up onto the former Holywell branch railway line. Soon cross a footbridge then continue on the wide trackbed up the wooded valley past waymarked side paths. *Built in 1869 to serve local quarries, the standard gauge branch line provided a passenger service from Greenfield until 1954. The 'Little Train', as it was known, steamed up a gradient of 1 in 27.* At a signposted junction keep ahead (Town Centre) past St Winefride's Halt to eventually pass under a road bridge at the site of the former Holywell station. Follow a meandering path up to Tesco's car park. Keep ahead, go through the underpass, up steps and along Tower Gardens to the High Street.

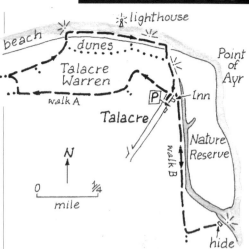

## WALK 26
# TALACRE

**DESCRIPTION** Two short walks near the mouth of the Dee Estuary. A 1¾ mile walk (**A**) featuring dunes, beach and a 19thC lighthouse. A 1½ mile walk (**B**) near Point of Ayr Nature Reserve, an important roosting site for wetland birds, to an RSPB hide. *Bring binoculars.* Allow about 1 hour.

**START** Car park by the Smuggler's Inn, Talacre [SJ 124848].

**DIRECTIONS** From the A548 follow the road into Talacre to the car park and inn just before its end.

**G***ronant Dunes and Talacre Warren SSSI is rich in plant, animal, bird and insect life. The land owned by BHP Billiton, which processes gas piped from platforms visible in Liverpool Bay, is managed with other agencies for nature conservation. A notable landmark is the lighthouse, built in 1819 to replace an earlier 1777 one. It had a flashing light with a range of 19 miles. It has survived a replacement 1844 iron tower, and a later tower built in 1891. Its subsequent uses have included a store, wartime lookout, and holiday home.*

**W**alk **A** Go to the road end, then take a cycle/walkway on the left signposted to Gronant into Gronant Dunes and Talacre Warren SSSI. Follow the wide surfaced recreational route for nearly ½ mile, then turn RIGHT on a concrete path signposted to the beach. Follow the waymarked permissive bridleway through the dunes onto the beach, or alternative waymarked black trail high tide option as shown. Head east past the lighthouse and a large finger post to leave the beach by a flagpole. Go across to a viewing platform on dunes ahead, past information boards, and along the embanked path to the road end.

**W**alk **B** Go to the road end and up to the Talacre Beach information board. Follow the path signposted to Ffynnongroyw/Bird Hide along the embankment, later passing the perimeter of BHP gas terminal, then bending left to the hide. Retrace your steps.

# PRONUNCIATION

| Welsh | English equivalent |
|---|---|
| c | always hard, as in cat |
| ch | as in the Scottish word loch |
| dd | as th in then |
| f | as f in of |
| ff | as ff in off |
| g | always hard as in got |
| ll | no real equivalent. It is like 'th' in then, but with an 'L' sound added to it, giving 'thlan' for the pronunciation of the Welsh 'Llan'. |

In Welsh the accent usually falls on the last-but-one syllable of a word.

## KEY TO THE MAPS

- ➖➤ Walk route and direction
- ═══ Metalled road
- ─ ─ ─ Unsurfaced road
- •••• Footpath/route adjoining walk route
- ∿∿⟶ River/stream
- ♣ ♤ Trees
- ▰▭▰ Railway
- **G** Gate
- **S** Stile
- **F.B.** Footbridge
- ☼ Viewpoint
- **P** Parking
- **T** Telephone

## THE COUNTRYSIDE CODE

- Be safe – plan ahead and follow any signs
- Leave gates and property as you find them
- Protect plants and animals, and take your litter home
- Keep dogs under close control
- Consider other people

**About the author, David Berry**

David is an experienced walker with a love of the countryside and an interest in local history. He is the author of a series of walks guidebooks covering North Wales, where he has lived and worked for many years, and been a freelance writer for Walking Wales magazine. He has also worked as a Rights of Way surveyor across North Wales and served as a member of Denbighshire Local Access Forum. For more information visit:

www.davidberrywalks.co.uk

Published by **Kittiwake-Books Limited**
3 Glantwymyn Village Workshops, Glantwymyn, Machynlleth, Montgomeryshire SY20 8LY
© Text & map research: David Berry 2012
© Maps & illustrations: Kittiwake 2012
*Drawings by* Morag Perrott
*Cover photos: Main* – The Groves, Chester. *Inset* – The Dee Estuary near Bettisfield. David Berry

Care has been taken to be accurate. However neither the author nor the publisher can accept responsibility for any errors which may appear, or their consequences. If you are in any doubt about access, check before you proceed.

Printed by MWL, Pontypool.
ISBN: **978 1 902302 99 7**